One Shall Chase a Thousand

One Shall Chase a Thousand

THE STORY OF MABEL FRANCIS

Mabel Francis

with Gerald B. Smith

Christian Publications
CAMP HILL, PENNSYLVANIA

Christian Publications
3825 Hartzdale Drive, Camp Hill, PA 17011

The mark of ✝ *vibrant faith*

ISBN: 0-87509-513-5
LOC Catalog Card Number: 93-70740
© 1993 by Christian Publications
All rights reserved
Printed in the United States of America

93 94 95 96 97 5 4 3 2 1

Cover illustration © 1993 by Karl Foster

Miss Mabel Francis

Anne Dievendorf and Mabel Francis leave the Hiroshima airport for retirement.

Miss Francis spoke at a Labor Day rally in Lima, Ohio in 1948. The young people of the Toledo Gospel Tabernacle presented her with this motor scooter.

Contents

Foreword 1

Prologue 2

1 *A Policeman at My Door* 5

2 *Sorting Out Your Loyalties* 9

3 *The Emperor's Newspaper* 4

4 *"Come Home!"* 19

5 *Important Influences* 24

6 *Good-Bye at a Young Man's Grave* 31

7 *Nyack via Brockton* 36

Interlude 42

8 *Japan at Last* 44

9 *Plain Words about the Self-Life* 51

10 *Genuine Conversions —* 58
Lasting Results

11 *The Ministry Comes to Me* 65

12 *Enemy Nationals* 69

13 "Tomorrow" 75

14 "Give Us Our Daily Bread" 80

15 The Emperor Ends the War 85

Interlude 90

16 America's Failure in Japan 93

17 Survivors 97

18 Hiroshima 104

19 A Special Place in My Heart 112

20 "The Weary Ladies" 118

Epilogue 124

Appendix I — A Legend in Her Time 128

Appendix II — Better Than a Fable 134

Appendix III — Interview 138

Appendix IV — Memories 144

Foreword

On the occasion of the celebration of 100 years of Alliance ministry in the "Land of the Rising Sun," it gives me great pleasure to write a foreword to *One Shall Chase a Thousand*.

Mabel Francis was here for more than 50 of those years. Whether in our churches or suffering in a Yokohama prison camp or in an audience with the Empress or other dignitaries, she preached Christ.

Miss Francis came to Japan with few worldly goods and left with the eternal wealth of hundreds of Japanese won to Christ. She received the highest honor the government ever bestowed on a foreigner. But beyond the praise of men, Miss Francis won the hearts of the Japanese people. A pastor once told me, "Mabel Francis was one of us!" That is the greatest compliment a missionary can receive.

Her preaching of Christ, her message of the Spirit-filled life, her deep love for the Japanese people and her sacrificial lifestyle still speak, though her lips are now silent. May her message speak to you through the pages of this book.

Richard C. Kropp
Field Director, Japan Alliance Mission
Tokyo, Japan

Prologue

It was the summer of 1945, just before the end of the great war in the Pacific, and the city of Tokyo was in ruins.

The long-range American bombers had become a scourge, spewing their destructive explosives on the Japanese cities, while desperate military and government leaders considered the few remaining alternatives to surrender.

Among the Japanese there was an impending sense of doom, but it could not be publicly confessed because of the traditions of super patriotism and "loss of face."

Gaunt and weary Americans, still surviving after four exhausting years in Japanese internment and prison camps within the environs of Tokyo, realized their danger, too, as the American B-29 bombers made their runs high in the skies over the Tokyo targets.

But Mabel Francis was an exception. She had no personal fear for herself, because she had chosen to stay in Japan during the war in order to be on the scene to help the Japanese people when the war ended. Although she turned 65 years of age in that summer of 1945, her thoughts did not stray towards the prospect of retirement. She thought only of the great spiritual and emotional needs of the Japanese when the disaster of defeat would finally come.

Miss Francis and her sister, Mrs. Anne Dievendorf, were two of the surviving Americans in Tokyo—and two of God's great missionary nobility. With hunger pressing in upon them daily, they were waiting out the end of the war in a Catholic monastery which the Japanese had pressed into service as an alien internment camp.

The fires and destruction resulting from the bombings seemed to creep closer and closer to the institution housing women internees from several nations at war with the Japanese. Nightly they were herded by their Japanese jailors into the basement, as the sirens wailed the signal of American bombers overhead.

Anne, the junior sister in terms of age, was often near the point of nervous exhaustion. She had been in camp detention since the day after the Pearl Harbor attack in 1941.

So it was not surprising that on one of those August nights in 1945, huddling in the cellar and with bombing targets leaping into flames nearby, Anne whispered, "Mabel, if they would make just one second's mistake in letting those bombs go, they would fall on us!"

But the senior sister had an amazing answer of faith for the terror of fear.

"Anne, that's one thing we don't have to be afraid of, for we know why we are here. We have been here all this time at God's command, and with His promise that 'one shall chase a thousand and two put ten thousand to flight.' It just wouldn't read right—that we stayed in Japan at God's command only to be killed by mistake in an American bombing raid!"

Faith was triumphant and the story does read right. And Mabel Francis is semi-retired at the age of 87, finally taking time off to tell it!

Written in 1968 by
Gerald B. Smith

1

A Policeman at My Door

I t did not seem possible that tiny Japan and the powerful United States of America could be on a collision course in 1941. But dark war clouds were hanging over Japan and I knew that I was under surveillance, for there was always a policeman stationed outside the door of my little missionary home in Matsuyama.

All Americans were suspects in Japan in those days prior to the attack on Pearl Harbor and the actual beginning of the war with America. It was a very hard time for missionaries. We couldn't do very much, we didn't have free access to travel and, worst of all, the Japanese people themselves were afraid to come to us, afraid to be seen talking with us. When the relations between the United States and Japan began deteriorating so rapidly in 1941, I had already been living in Japan for 32 years. The board of The Christian and Missionary Alliance in New York had altered its policy in 1909 to allow me, as a single woman, to sail for Japan to join the small missionary forces in these islands.

My brother, the Rev. Thomas Francis, had left an Alliance pastorate in New Jersey to come to Japan in 1913. He had enjoyed a very successful missionary career which emphasized the launching of new Mission churches. In 1941 however, he was home on furlough.

My sister, Anne, who had joined me in Japan in 1922 after the death of her husband, was located in the strategic city of Fujuyama on the large island of Honshu. I was on the other side of the Inland Sea, in the city of Matsuyama on the island of Shikoku.

Our missionary work had brought us very close to the hearts of many of the Japanese people and we knew that, as a whole, the people themselves did not want war. If it had been left to the people, war with all of its horror and death and destruction would not have been their will.

I had a number of Japanese friends living with me at that time and they felt worse about it than I did. But if any of them dared to say a word against the prospect of war, they would pay for it.

We must remember that, at that point in history, the Japanese government and military figures were very proud, having gained a great victory over China and over Russia before that. The leaders had come to the place where they thought they could fight the whole world and win. They had carefully prepared for this and they thought they would emerge victorious.

Now I don't think my American loyalty will come into question if I say a word about the American-Japanese relations in those years preceding World War II.

Living as I did in Japan during that time, I believe that we, as a great American nation, had become very coarse in our dealing with these Orientals who are of such a deeply sensitive nature. This doesn't excuse Japan, by any means, but we have something to think about as we look back on it.

I think the troubles began with the immigration problems. The United States originally had a covenant with Japan—a gentleman's agreement—in which Japan promised to send only "suitable" people to America. The Japanese government felt that it had kept the agreement and could not understand the reason for sudden restrictive quotas being announced by the American government.

The restrictive quotas apparently were announced by the United States without any consultation with the Japanese. They were terribly upset and felt they had lost face and had been affronted by the Americans.

From that time on we began to hear them say, "We've just got to fight with America! We've just got to show them that we are not as dumb as they think we are!" This became a deep conviction in their hearts.

It was not the American people, either, who had taken the action, but it was the government. We missionaries in Japan felt very sad about it, for it gave opportunity for the Japanese people to think undue ill thoughts about us.

And then, of course, it was one thing after another. You know how it is when feelings get hurt—it's like having a sensitive toe out there and everything strikes it. So one thing added to another to further strain the relations.

No one had to come and tell me personally that the government was upset with Americans. The policeman posted outside my door was message enough.

One day he told me that war with the United States would break out very soon.

"Oh, no!" I said to him. "Don't let them do it! You have no idea how large and strong America is."

"I know," he answered, "but I think we can do it."

I kept it to myself, for he would have suffered if it had become known that he had told an American even that much. And, for a policeman, he had actually been very kind to me.

2

Sorting Out Your Loyalties!

I have had many people in the churches at home say to me, "Didn't you just feel like getting up and running away from Japan when it seemed that war was certain?"

In spite of the fact that I was an American and treasured my own national citizenship, I had only one reason for being in Japan.

God had called me, when I was a young woman, to be His ambassador in Japan. The calling of God to be a Christian missionary is not something incidental. I can relate God's definite dealing with me about Christian service to the faith and prayers of my mother in a small New Hampshire community three-quarters of a century ago.

Mother was a woman of deep faith. She was quiet and gentle, and faithfully taught the family about the things of God. We children were raised with the constant vision of our mother weeping over the lost in all the lands around the world.

Although it has been 80 years and more since that time, I can actually remember being so moved by these times of intercession on the part of my mother that I would say to her, "Don't cry, Mother, and don't worry! When I grow up, I will tell the world all about Jesus."

From the time that I was a little child, I had the inward certainty that I would be a missionary some day. Is this something that we have lost in our advanced day—the calling of God, a vision and realization put before us in the spiritual ministry of our parents in the home?

Memories of the living God at work in your own childhood can be a most vital source of spiritual strength and encouragement when you have been separated from home and loved ones and country and comforts in order to tell people of the love of Jesus!

I still have the strongest recollection of Mother and Father and members of our family in daily prayers. Father would lead in a song, read the Scriptures and then he would pray. All of us would join in the Lord's Prayer at the end of each family altar period.

I am sure that it was almost daily in this childhood period of my life that I had this feeling: "Our house is a safe house, with Father praying and with Mother trusting the Lord. How can there be any safety for people who do not pray?" There were seven children in the family. I was the third.

I became a schoolteacher in my teens and then had opportunity as a girl preacher to witness the gospel to many communities in New Hampshire and Massachusetts.

Through this evangelistic activity, I was called to

Haverhill, Massachusetts, to conduct meetings. I had such a growing concern for the work of missions and the need of the lost that I prayed, "O God, talk to the hearts of the people about missions and let something really happen this time. Call someone out!"

There happened to be a missionary couple from Japan speaking in their farewell service in the church and I went to the altar with others. It was I whom God called!

There was such pressure upon me for the will of God that I actually bled from the nose and mouth. I saw a vision of the islands of Japan and the Japanese people. I was about 19 at the time of this call.

I told my mother, "God has called me to Japan."

I can never forget how she wept. It seemed so unusual to me that one could weep such tears of joy.

She said, "Mabel, you know how I love Japan, but I could never go myself. I am happy that you can go and your being in Japan will be a great joy to me."

This was my youthful preparation for missionary work and service for Christ.

Through the auspices of Dr. A.B. Simpson and The Christian and Missionary Alliance, God brought me to Japan in 1909.

I struggled with the Japanese language, and though it was so difficult to learn, I had an unusual joy in the process, for I would remind myself of the day that I could begin to use it to communicate with these most interesting people. They were to become the people of my adoption. That is why I did not feel like running to safety when the dangers first became apparent in 1941.

Even though I had come to talk and to think and to act very much like my Japanese neighbors during those 32 years, I knew that the Japanese leaders were wrong. God knew it, too. I knew they were doing something they had no business to do. But I also knew that God's love for them did not change because of that. I was not there to judge them but to teach them of the love of God. During the war itself, I could not rejoice when Japan gained a victory because I knew they were wrong.

You see, my loyalty to Japan is not like the loyalty to my own country. I am loyal to Japan because God loves the Japanese people. It was not even because of my own love for the Japanese that I stayed, but because God loved them. It was not a nationalistic loyalty to Japan that kept me there.

Before Pearl Harbor, I was able to keep in touch with my sister Anne. Our mail was censored, but we could write to each other. We encouraged each other to search the Scriptures and to pray for the will of God.

Even though we could not get together for a conference, the Lord spoke to each of us. Suppose we were to come to a time of testing, a time of persecution, a time of danger? Both of us agreed in heart and mind and being.

For our missionary work, God spoke out of Isaiah 45: "I will give you the treasures of darkness, riches stored in secret places." For our personal strength and assurance, He spoke out of Deuteronomy 32: "One shall chase a thousand, or two shall put ten thousand to flight."

The American consul advised us to leave Japan. Friends wrote us and gave kind advice to "pick up and come away now, for we don't know what's going to happen." But we were not just American tourists visiting in Japan.

The Lord said to me, "War cannot break out until I permit it, and when I do permit it, I will take care of you. There is no need to fear."

3

The Emperor's Newspaper

Any American living as I did in Japan during the preparation for the war in the Pacific would have been struck again and again by the great difference between American ideas and Japanese ideas and by the manner in which the military clique was able to sweep even the Emperor himself along with the proposition that war was inevitable.

The men high in the Japanese government had made up their minds that war had to come—and they deceived the Emperor. They told him Japan was being surrounded by the Americans, the British, the Chinese and the Dutch—the "ABCD" encirclement.

Now, I think the events at the end of the war and Japan's history since the war have given the world the very definite indication of the many fine qualities and character of the Emperor.

One of the important things that happened prior to the war and even during the early stages of the war was the deceitful manipulation of the

Emperor's personal newspaper. It was a special newspaper printed just for the Emperor himself. So the government leaders doctored up the reports and put into the Emperor's newspaper the things they wanted him to see. They persuaded him that if the Japanese did not strike very soon, other nations would strike and Japan would be destroyed. He, of course, not knowing anything else, supposed it to be true. That's how they got him to declare war.

It was not too long after I arrived in Japan in 1909 that the country was opened to outside influences. After getting off the boat in Yokohama, I was struck by the completely new world into which I had stepped as an American.

The first thing that struck me was the hopelesness on the faces of the older people. They seemed to be looking out into space—no brightness, no hope there. Japan at that point was still almost untouched by western civilization.

Through the years, I saw a great many occasions for sorrow and grief and suffering in Japan. Fires, floods, disease—and, of course, the great earthquake in 1923.

I mention these calamities and disasters against the background of the inevitable great war in the Pacific because those who lived in Japan know full well the secret of Japan's amazing rise as a military power. The philosophy of the common people of the country was that those who died fighting for the Emperor would immediately be dispatched into an eternal paradise of bliss.

One American who was returning to live in Japan after the great earthquake recalled his conversation with a Japanese youth carrying his baggage from the station.

"But, sir, the earthquake was worse than war because all soldiers who die fighting for the Emperor ascend to bliss, while we don't know what happens to the poor souls who died in the disaster," the boy said.

He put his finger right on the hopelessness of the crowds which continually thronged the little tin-roofed wooden shrines where the bones of earthquake victims reposed.

Perhaps this makes it easier for you to see and understand the suicide pilots and suicide squads of Japanese who gave their full devotion to their Emperor and the Japanese ideal during World War II.

Through my early years of ministry in Japan, I became fully aware of the many ways in which the sensitive Japanese people were trained and expected to worship other gods and other ideas. One had only to see the thousands who worshiped spirits of departed soldiers at the magnificent Yasukuni Shrine in Tokyo coming away with their heads held high, proud that their families had contributed sons in the Emperor's service. The souls of all the faithful who died in the service of their country were enshrined there. It was one of the places which had become a symbol of the spirit which made modern Japan.

By 1914 Japan's efficient army and navy had brought the island empire to the position of being the most powerful country in East Asia.

During World War I, Japan took advantage of

Germany's situation to occupy German colonies in the island chains of the Pacific. Thus they had an empire stretching from the ice-bound Kurile Islands to the equator and from the coast of China to the international dateline in the mid-Pacific.

In the Washington Armament Conference in 1922, the United States, Britain, France and Japan all agreed to respect each other's rights in their island possessions and promised not to build any fortifications on these islands. America, Britain and Japan also agreed to limit the size of their navies.

When World War II finally came, it was apparent that Japan had secretly begun to fortify the most important of her island possessions. She had also built more and bigger ships than the Washington Naval Treaty permitted. By 1940, Japan's influence in China had become a war of conquest which was then followed by the military occupation of French Indo-China.

You will remember that the United States warned Japan in August 1941 that further aggression would be met by the United States with "any and all steps necessary." President Roosevelt stopped all American trade with Japan, cutting off most of the oil and steel needed by Japanese war industries.

So in October 1941 the new Japanese prime minister, General Hideki Tojo, began plans for an early war against the United States. The Japanese army then had the strength of 2.4 million men. There were also 3 million men in the trained reserves and Japan's navy and air forces were large, efficient and ready for war.

Small wonder then that my friends in the United States wrote urgently, "Come home now—come home while you can!"

But Anne and I agreed, in our occasional letters, that we had a definite word from the Lord and His distinct promises. We were in Japan not at the command of a person, nor of the consul, but at the command of God. So He was the One to tell us what to do. As we prayed and looked to Him, He showed us so clearly that now was the time to stand.

This was why He had brought us to Japan—to show forth His love to these people. To pick up everything and go away when things became difficult would not show His love. We knew we must stay. We settled it in our hearts—to do the will of God was primary. Whether we lived or died was secondary.

Now it may sound very strange to some folks in our modern day and age to say that we heard the voice of God, that we knew by His Word and by His Spirit what He wanted us to do. I am not at all embarrassed to tell you that from childhood I have earnestly sought the guidance of the living God by His Spirit and by His Word day by day.

I feel sorry for those who have only doubts and criticisms and who have never known in their lives the sweet, still, small voice of the Spirit of God deep within their beings. I grieve for what they are missing in life's most blessed experience of walking day by day with the Lord Jesus Christ.

4

"Come Home!"

Having made my decision that Japan was the place for me, regardless of the threat of war and the certain privations of a prison camp, I suddenly realized that the Lord had led me over this same ground before.

Surely no one ought to be surprised that I was remaining in Japan to be near the Japanese people. I had made this unreserved decision once before, when The Christian and Missionary Alliance had found it necessary to withdraw from Japan early in the years of the Great Depression at home.

I was a missionary with more than 20 years of residence in Japan when the word came from the Foreign Department offices of the Alliance in New York that, due to the Depression and a number of discouraging circumstances on the field, the Alliance felt it best to withdraw from Japan. This meant, the message said, that the missionaries would be expected to come home and, if possible, to be reassigned to other fields.

Well, I don't remember whether it was a cloudy day when the letter came, but the rest of the day was gray, I can tell you. I was alone on the island at

the time with both my sister and brother in the
States on furlough. So I had to seek the Lord alone
for the answer.

As I thought about it, I reminded myself that my
greatest aim had been that God should be
glorified. I thought back over God's dealing with
me particularly in the two years just prior to the call
to return home. I had just had the vision that if I
could get through to the place where I had a single
eye for the glory of God, where self was on the
cross and Christ on the throne, that He would be
glorified here in the land of Japan.

But then everything turned dark.

I tried to go to prayer and wait before the Lord,
but I don't think I prayed very much at first. I was
just silent before the Lord. And then I began to
pray that He would show me what I was to do.

I thought, "Well, if the board calls me home, how
can I stay here? I wouldn't have any money, for a
board couldn't continue to support me if I was disobedient to their commands."

This seemed to be the end. I knew that it
wouldn't be proper for a missionary to go out and
take up a remunerative job. I couldn't see that that
would be for the glory of God.

So the question continued, "What shall I do?"

And, oh, how the pressures came upon me! What
a thought—the thought of going back home to
stay, of leaving Japan forever.

Day after day and night after night I sat or lay
and thought, "What shall I do? What is God's will
for me? I have come this far with a divine command over me. Now what shall I do?"

The agony got deeper and deeper. It would be impossible to really tell anyone what I went through during those days. I considered what it would mean to give up my evangelistic work in Matsuyama as evangelist, working with Pastor Ogata, and traveling in country areas, too, wherever the churches called.

The letter from the board was rather an ultimatum, because it pointed out that certain decisions had already been made and that the withdrawal from Japan was already decided. There were no negotiations. There was nothing to talk about.

Pastor Ogata and the other national pastors had also received the word by this time that the Mission would leave Japan. They were very upset by this word. There is probably a letter in an old Japan file at the national office because the pastors wrote one expressing their sorrow that the missionaries would be moved on. There were about 20 churches at that time.

I can see now, in my mind's eye, my empty trunk, for I had emptied everything out. I had thought that I would have to get things packed, but I don't think I ever got more than two items in the trunk.

I was not living in a very good house at that time—in fact, I had never had in Japan what we would consider an American house. I had moved many times and this last one was rather a poor place. It did have an upstairs, however. So I would go up and start on the trunk and my hands would just drop at my side. I couldn't go on. I would go back to my room and begin to pray again.

One day, after I had been out calling, I came home with a heart as heavy as lead, thinking again, "What shall I do?"

It was then that I heard a voice in my soul. Actually, at the time it was so vivid that I thought I was hearing it with my natural ears: "Would you fear to stay here and just trust Me, even if the board does withdraw?"

I knew it was the voice of God and I looked up and said, "Lord, you know I have told you that I will do whatever you want."

He spoke to me again: "You know that I have called you to Japan—that is even before the board's call. And the work I wanted you to do is not yet finished. I want you to stay here."

I remember that I was frightened. I was still young at the time and my future life seemed to be threatened if I stayed in Japan with no home church or organization or board to back me.

I said to the Lord, "But if I live to be 70 years old, everyone in America will forget that I exist and I might starve right here."

And then the Lord said, "If I let you live to be 70. . . ."

I needed to hear that to make me realize that my life was completely in His hands. His promise was, "I will not forget you."

I knew then what God wanted me to do and it was settled in my soul.

"Heavenly Father," I prayed, "it is settled. I will stay here."

Suddenly, all of the burden and uncertainty lifted. It was gone! And such a joy filled my soul.

The next morning when I walked out for the morning prayer meeting, it seemed to me that even my feet, as they touched the Japanese soil, were actually singing in answer to the will of God.

Everything was settled. Although the Alliance board had felt its own leading and direction from the Lord for the withdrawal, I had to resign and advise them of my own leading to stay in Japan to do the work God had called me to do.

This experience in 1934 was a unique preparation for the decision that had to be made again in 1941—the decision to stay and complete the work still unfinished.

5

Important Influences

Japan is like any other country where human beings live. If you are going to be of help, you must be prepared to deal with spiritual darkness and immoral conditions existing against the background of worship of many gods.

People have said to me many times when I have been home on furlough: "You must have been a brave girl to start out for Japan alone in 1909."

After all of these years at work on the field, let me tell you that missionary work is not just "another job"—it is serious business and you won't fit into a situation in any country unless you have walked definitely in the leading of the Lord and know for sure that He has placed you in the right place at the right time.

God will have His own way of preparing you spiritually and mentally and physically, too, for the many unusual problems you will face in a different country and in an unusual culture.

When I first arrived in Japan in 1909, I came in contact with Miss Christine Penrod, who was running a most effective rescue mission near the famous licensed prostitution area in Tokyo. Everyone that knew her said, "Well, there's a character for you!"

Miss Penrod was big and strong and never wore a hat. She carried a man's umbrella to keep the sun off her head. She also didn't hesitate to stand up to the men of the red-light district. I had known her since my childhood because she was a member of my father's denomination and whenever she was home on furlough she would come to speak.

I thought when I had been in Japan a little while and had seen the awful conditions that maybe God wanted me to work with her. I went up to Tokyo thinking that perhaps I would join her, but I soon felt that it was not my place.

There were so many women—really lovely women—who had not gone into sin, but who were just as much lost as these people were. I told Miss Penrod of my decision, and she said, "All right."

I have no reason to think that I could have stayed in Japan and continued to love the people there and to accomplish the work of God if I had refused the Lord's dealing with me even when I was a child.

My father was ordained by the Christian Church when I was about eight years old. We lived in Grafton, New Hampshire, and Father served a circuit of three churches which had been considered "empty" churches. The church which Father built at Grafton is still there.

The education of the family was of considerable importance to my parents. There was a Literary Institute at New Hampton and Father said that

Mother should move over to New Hampton with the children so that we older ones could go to school.

We came in contact there with a Christian family who were known as "holiness people." I was about 14 years old and when I saw the blessedness of their victory and freedom in the things of God, I became hungry in my own spirit and began to seek.

I remember praying, "Lord, unless you give me the assurance of a clean heart, I am never going to come out of this room."

As I continued to pray and seek, it was as though someone put a hand on my shoulder and as though I heard a voice from heaven saying, "The blood of Jesus Christ, God's Son, cleanseth us from all sin."

Thus I came to know the blessedness of complete surrender to the will of God and I received the Holy Spirit.

You see, I knew my need for Christian victory. During this time Mother had been taking care of my father during a serious illness. I had to take care of my brother and sister and I often became impatient. I often scolded and spanked them and sensed so keenly the personal need to know the real blessing of forgiveness and victory and compassion. These came to me as realities when the Holy Spirit came to dwell in me and to guide me.

It was during these years that my father started taking the members of our family to the Old Orchard Camp of The Missionary Alliance in Maine. Dr. A.B. Simpson was coming to the fore in his missionary work and his summer conventions became very well known throughout New England.

Because we had to make the trip to the camp in our horse-drawn carriage, we could not all go at the same time. Each year Father would take several of us and I remember we had a very slow, old horse. The trip would take two days and we generally stopped with someone overnight. Because of the distance, Father planned the trip so that we stayed for the duration of the camp.

Many people stayed in tents at Old Orchard, although there were some cottages. I recall that we had an upstairs room in a cottage.

The camp sessions were geared to adult listeners, but the children were expected to attend the sessions. There was no planned program of recreation. I know that I got sleepy many times, but I was interested in the gospel messages and tried to listen attentively.

I remember very well the times of unusual blessing and the moving of the Holy Spirit. There were times when women attending the camp would get up and take off their jewelry and put it in the offering for missions.

I recall one lady so overwhelmed by the message of the gospel to the lost that she put everything in the offering that she had—money and jewelry—and then she shouted, "If the basket were larger, I would get in myself!"

Because the Lord has given me this long life and I can still remember the associations with Dr. A.B. Simpson, let me share a few impressions about this man of God who could not rest until he felt that he was doing all he could in every way for the evangelization of the world for Jesus Christ.

Dr. Simpson was a rather large man, physically. He had broad shoulders. When he came into the room or to the platform, it seemed as though a spiritual giant had entered. As he spoke or taught, you knew that you were in the presence of a man of God. The more you were in his presence, the more you came to realize that this was truly a self-effacing man.

At Old Orchard Dr. Simpson was always full of a burden and love for lost souls. He was always thoughtful of others, particularly of missionaries who attended the services. I do recall, too, that in spite of his burden and serious attitude about the lost, he would often chuckle within himself as he preached, especially when he was telling what God was doing or what God was able to do in His world in response to faith.

Dr. Simpson was a good organizer and a good planner. You could tell this in his meetings and you could tell it in his presentation of missionary projects. He never spoke of missionary projects in terms of great international problems representing hundreds of thousands of dollars. He always broke them down so that his listeners could get hold and take part.

For instance, I remember in the early presentation of the mission to Tibet that it was rather a grand undertaking for those days, and yet Dr. Simpson broke it down so that many were willing to take a $25 share in getting the Tibetan project underway.

But with good organization, good planning and presentation, those who listened and participated with Dr. Simpson, in those days, recognized that it was still all the work of the Holy Spirit.

At Old Orchard, of course, the meetings were all outdoors. There were benches under the trees and there was always sincere prayer about the weather in connection with the blessing of God on the convention. Only once in my memory of Old Orchard was there rain at the time of a scheduled service.

Dr. Simpson would take a missionary pledge and he always accompanied this with rich, spiritual teaching and exhortation. After all these years, I can remember so well one of the occasions when Dr. Simpson used the words, "On His Heart, In His Hands, At His Feet and At His Command."

Let me say this about sacrificing for the Christian gospel and missionary work. As Dr. Simpson dealt with the Word of God and its teachings of the command to go with the gospel and the need of the heathen, Christian people in his audiences did not seem to think of their giving in terms of sacrifice. People actually came hundreds of miles just to see Dr. Simpson receive the missionary offering. He had a pleasing, melodious voice and the meetings were permeated with a sense of joy. The music of choruses and songs always seemed to be in the Spirit.

There were miraculous healings that took place from time to time. The emphasis of those who were brought into the work with Dr. Simpson seemed to be that they were not holding anything back, but were gladly giving everything for Jesus and the lost world.

Dr. Simpson always looked cleanly dressed, with

a tie and a clean collar, but with a suit not always in the latest fashion of his day. I do remember that he wore a suit which was shiny almost to the point of being green—you know how black can get when it is worn—but it was pressed, and he didn't care about things like that. He was all out for God.

Those who have memories of Dr. A.B. Simpson will agree with me that he was a man who always seemed to have an audience with the King and gave a sense of intimate communion with the Lord. He encouraged others to simple, godly habits, always with the emphasis that wherever we were placed, we were always to be known and used as ambassadors for God.

I also remember Mrs. Simpson, particularly as she would cross the campus at Nyack, New York, at the Missionary Institute. Once, during a meeting, she said to me. "I just had nothing else to put on but this black silk blouse. Do you think anyone will be stumbled by my wearing it?"

I assured her that it looked fine and I was sure that no one would be offended because Mrs. Simpson was wearing a silk blouse!

6

Good-Bye at a Young Man's Grave

God leads us all to His highest will by different routes. In most of our lives He will show us things to which we are holding, as though we know better than He what is most important. When we are young, sometimes falling in love seems to us to be the most important thing.

While we were living in New Hampshire, Mother rented out some rooms of the cottage. One of the renters was a young man who was ill with tuberculosis. My heart went out to him. I presume that it could be said that I developed a deep attachment to him. Some would undoubtedly say we were in love.

Well, he was the schoolteacher back at his home in Tamworth, New Hampshire. When his condition became worse, he asked Mother to bring me over to Tamworth to take up the teaching in his school.

I did not feel qualified at my age, but he said, "You start and I will help you if necessary." So, I taught school near Tamworth when I was still in my teens.

The young man did not recover from his serious illness. He was buried in a plot near the rural school where I taught. In fact, looking out of the schoolhouse, I could see the grave.

Each day I would take time to decorate the grave; and I am sure, now, that I felt very, very sorry for myself. I know that I was despondent and it was very apparent to those around me. But the Lord is faithful. He spoke to me so definitely one day as I made my usual trip to visit the grave.

"You are the only one in this village who has experienced my love and knows the Savior," He said to me. "Why do you weep over this young man who has gone on to heaven? You must tell the people of Tamworth that you know my love, and that they should also know it."

How glad I am that I listened to the voice of the Spirit of God.

I invited everyone in the community to come to the schoolhouse one Sunday afternoon. Since there was no other church service in the area, nearly everyone came to the meeting. I told them in the best way I could of God's love and His plan of salvation through Christ, and did we have a revival!

We continued the meetings. I recall the hard-handed old farmers, with their smell of tobacco, being moved for God. The news of this spiritual movement soon became known in the village of Tamworth, and the minister came to see me.

"I want you to come down and give your testimony to the women of my church," he said. I was about 17 years old then.

There were many opportunities to give my testimony and I would take my brother Tom, who would sing. My mother was always anxious about what I would be led to say in a meeting, but the Lord worked in all of these schoolhouse meetings. Generally, the schools were filled with people from the neighborhood and inasmuch as I testified to the plan of salvation and the faithfulness of God and the need of lost souls, we generally had souls saved.

One village after another called for me in those teen years to testify and speak about the Christian gospel. We had a big revival in South Tamworth and many lives were transformed. We had similar meetings and revivals in Sanburnton, Meredith and other New Hampshire communities.

It was after this, when I was 19, that I was called to Haverhill, Massachusetts, and had the experience of a definite call to work for God in Japan. I knew then that I must complete my schooling in order to be ready for God's plan for my life. So I registered at the Gordon Bible School, which is now Gordon College, in Boston. The school was associated then with the Clarendon Street Church in Boston where one of my uncles, Dr. James Francis, was pastor.

I had made up my mind that I would ask no one for any financial help in the final stages of my preparation for the Lord's work. When I arrived in Boston, I had money only to pay for one week's room rent. It was my very strong impression that I should know how to intimately trust the Lord for my needs in America, before I should become committed to trusting Him for my needs in Japan. Along with this impression, I felt that I should tell no one about my finances.

The first week in Boston went by rapidly and I knew that it would soon be time to pay my rent again. I spent a great deal of time in prayer at night, with concern and weeping, as I reminded the Lord of my need. On Friday, just before the rent had to be paid—in fact, the landlady had already mentioned it—I received a letter from a lady quite a distance away. She enclosed $12.50, and said in the letter, "I don't know where you are now, so I am sending this letter to your father so he can forward it to you."

While this certainly was an answer to prayer, it was also a rebuke to my impatience in faith. I said within myself, "Here you have been crying and weeping and showing such concern night after night about the rent coming due and the Lord had this money on the way and in the mail all this time."

I got down again to pray. "Lord, I have learned my lesson. I am committed to trusting you for my needs every day and you know all about them. I promise that I will not cry and fret again as I have this week about the rent money."

There were other times of testing during this period at school. There were days when there was very little to eat. I remember that there were times when I had only beans and cornmeal with no sugar or salt. But I was learning the valuable and important lessons of being able to trust the Lord and to experience joy and contentment with His will.

While I was in school at Boston, a gentleman from Brockton, Massachusetts, came to me and said, "Will you come to Brockton and preach for us next Sunday?"

I am not sure that he knew about my precarious financial arrangement, but the Lord must have spoken to him, because he said, "You will need something for your fare." He gave me cash for more than the amount of the fare.

This allowed me to have a good meal so that I was physically reinforced before going to Brockton for the Sunday services. I used as my text an appropriate Old Testament verse: "Bread shall be given him, and his water shall be sure" (Isaiah 33:16, KJV).

7

Nyack via Brockton

Brockton was a shoe factory town, and when I sensed the low tide of moral and spiritual conditions there, God spoke to me very definitely and said, "I want you to start a rescue mission in Brockton."

Well, I was just a young girl, a Bible school student who had been invited to speak in a Brockton church. I had no official board to stand with me, no extension committee to encourage me by providing funds. But I felt that I must obey the leading of the Lord.

So I went to Brockton and rented a building with a store front and lived in a room in the rear of the building.

When I have told about this experience at times, I have had to answer the question, "Who paid the rent?"

Truthfully, the only answer I can give is, "Why, God, of course!"

I can assure you that there were continued times of testing of faith in the work of the Mission at Brockton. I had to continue often in prayer for the Lord's direction for the ministries we had there and about the month-to-month needs of the Mission.

I recall at one time when we were coming up to the end of the month. I knew that I would need $40 the next day for the rent. During a season of prayer, it seemed as though the Lord suddenly gave me a vision of a horse shying away from something in the road, but there was nothing there.

Then the Lord spoke to me: "Why don't you just rest in My promises and really trust Me?" The Spirit of God said within me, "You are shying away from nothing. I am looking out for the rest."

Again, I yielded in faith and the money I needed came in from an unexpected source the next day.

The Lord had a reason for my being in Brockton during those two years, 1900 and 1901. I had a most rewarding ministry as a Christian young woman because of the needs of so many girls who came to us out of their drunken and immoral lives.

The Lord made gracious provision in many ways for us to assist them and to bring them back to a life of respect and hope. Often we had to deal with unfriendly and ugly men who did their best to trace the girls whom we had assisted to slip out of their clutches. It was a most vivid experience in dealing with sinful humans so desperately in need of the love and grace of God.

One of the great names in the ministerial history of The Christian and Missionary Alliance is that of Dr. Ira David. It was during this time in Brockton that I became friends with the Davids. For many years Dr. David had a great impact on the spiritual life and teaching of the Alliance. At that time, he was pastor of the Alliance church in Brockton.

Both Dr. and Mrs. David were of great encouragement in the mission work we had ventured to do for the Lord and in my spiritual preparation for future missionary service in Japan.

In the summer of 1901, when I was 21, I went again to the camp at Old Orchard, Maine. On Saturday, a missionary showed pictures and included some slides of the Missionary Training Institute at Nyack, New York.

Even as I saw the pictures, God said to me, "You should be going there."

I whispered to the Lord, "I can't possibly go to school at Nyack because I do have responsibility for the Mission at Brockton and I don't have money to start school again."

But the Lord doesn't generally give you the last word in such a conversation as this.

I walked out to the pump after the meeting to get a drink of water before going to the train to return to Brockton. There was a lady at the pump. I don't really know who she was, except that her name was Mrs. Rose.

After we had a drink together, she said, "I have been watching you and I think you ought to be in school at Nyack."

I had to confess to her then how the Lord had started to deal with me and of the barriers that I felt were in the way.

Mrs. Rose then said to me, "If God shows you clearly that you should go to Nyack, I want you to know that the Lord has spoken to me and I will pay your tuition."

I was soon on the train back to Brockton and to

the Mission. I went to see Dr. and Mrs. David to tell them how the Lord was dealing with me. We prayed together for God's guidance.

I guess when we tell a story of how things were, we ought to tell the whole story. So this is a confession of a kind.

Actually, I was afraid to go to Nyack because I was not sure that I was in agreement with the teachings at the Institute. You see, I was still under the impressions of my holiness contacts from some years before. At that time I believed that holiness came by the process of eradication and that biblical sanctification was a result of eradication of the old human nature.

As much as I had enjoyed the Old Orchard camp meetings and Dr. Simpson's ministry and missionary emphasis, I was not sure that the Alliance was straight on the doctrine of sanctification.

I began to pray and to seek the Lord for direction concerning the future of the rescue mission. As always, God went before and worked out the things that seemed to me to be real problems and barriers. He provided for the leadership of the Mission and, when I was about 23, I registered at the Missionary Training Institute.

At Nyack I had opportunity to experience and become a part of the great revival which spread over the campus in the early years of the 20th century. I recall a period of three weeks of revival meetings on the campus when the Lord prevailed upon our hearts in such a way that there were no classes. Students were under deep conviction for their personal lives and ministry. There were many sessions of confession with resulting restitutions, and the tide of victory swept over the campus with songs and blessing day and night.

Let me caution you here that I have learned that little things—things that we say to ourselves are so small that they don't matter—are still things that can impede spiritual progress and keep us from the will of God.

On the closing baccalaureate Sunday of my senior year at Nyack, one of the young men working his way through school by cleaning and working in the bakery said that he must confess a wrongdoing.

He said that while cleaning in the school bakery, he was hungry and took a loaf of hot, freshly baked bread. He said he knew it would not be good for his digestion to eat the whole hot loaf, so he "skinned it" and ate the crust.

As he confessed this act and his need before the student body and the faculty, weeping broke out all over the chapel and God smote one after another so that there was a real breaking-up. One of the teachers, who was to preach the sermon, spoke just one sentence, "Today, if ye hear His voice, harden not your hearts. . . ." The weeping broke out again. This revival continued for a number of weeks, even though school was out. The effects were still felt as The Christian and Missionary Alliance General Council came to meet on the campus that year.

I felt that my academic work must be strengthened further before I went to Japan, so I enrolled at Defiance College which was related to my father's church. I wanted to find out the theological position of missionaries of the Christian Church, and so I wrote personally to one of them.

"Do the missionaries stand for the Bible?" I asked.

The answer came back, "Some do and some don't. After all, who can tell what is truth?"

I knew then that this was not the missionary climate in which I should work.

When I was 28, with all of this background of ministering and Bible training and academic studies, I told Dr. Simpson I was ready to go to the foreign field and that Japan was to be my field of service.

Interlude

Alliance churches seemed far apart, money was scarce and a deadline for sailing for Japan was near for Miss Mabel Francis in the summer of 1909.

Having declared herself to be a missionary candidate, she was asked by the Alliance Mission board to raise the necessary funds for her outfit, for her passage and for a year's support on the field.

There was no airplane to speed her from church to church, but there was the reality of prayer. What was a difficult task was not an impossible task for one who could truthfully say again and again, "God spoke to me. . . ."

So it was as though an unseen hand took Mabel's financial affairs in control.

"Almost every letter I received," Miss Francis recalls, "had some money in it." This went into the bank for the rail fare to Seattle and the steamship fare to Yokohama. Then it overflowed into the rather modest sum necessary for a year's support in Japan in 1909.

And how about the outfit for the missionary?

A lady in New Jersey gave Mabel three new gingham dresses to take to the field and, with the addition of a knife, a fork and a spoon, her personal outfit was complete.

"However, when I got to Japan," Mabel continues, "I could only wear two of the three dresses, because one was a black-and-white check, a color which turned out to be worn only by men in Japan."

She did have a little steamer trunk in which she packed her dresses, some books, some pictures and mementos of her family.

No one ever said anything to Mabel during this preparation about a furlough that would bring her back to the States.

"As far as I was concerned," she admits, "I was leaving home to go to Japan to spend the rest of my life."

Was this spiritually minded, 29-year-old, little New England woman actually human?

Oh, yes!

"In the bottom of my trunk I had a half-pound package of Baker's cocoa, and I felt a thrust of regret that when it was gone in Japan, it would be the last I would ever see!"

Mabel's mother used a horse and buggy to take her to the station at Westport, Massachusetts, in October, 1909. She arrived in Yokohama on November 30.

8

Japan at Last

No one could ever write a truthful book on missionary life and say that there are no crosses to bear, no disciplines, no frustrations, no disappointments.

I found them in Japan. You will find them wherever you go. But the blessed answer is in the presence of Christ, who said, "I will never leave you nor forsake you." If you go without His presence and the abiding reality of His Spirit, you will soon come home.

The Alliance work in Japan was very small when I arrived in 1909. There were just two small congregations, one in Nagoya and the other in Hiroshima. Rev. and Mrs. Hjalmer Lindstrom were the leaders in the Mission and were assisted by one other woman at that time. I went to Hiroshima with the Lindstroms and began to study the language immediately.

At that time in Japan the people would not think of wearing any foreign clothes. The men, for instance, did not wear business suits as they do now. The little children all wore bright-colored kimonos and everyone wore clogs with the strap running up between the toes.

Passing down the street, you could look into the homes and everyone, of course, was sitting on the floor. There were no chairs. Although I was an American missionary, I soon became one of the Japanese in many ways. I had no furniture and used the floor for most things just as the Japanese do. I had no heat in the winter season in what is called a house—but certainly not a house in the same sense as in America. I cooked on an earthen hibachi, the type of charcoal stove used by the people in their homes.

I rode a bicycle everywhere. Although motor buses came into use later in Japan, I had to stick with my bicycle. Often, when the buses would pass me on the road, I would think how nice it would be to have money to ride the bus. Riding the bicycle up and down the roads and trails and hills was a trying experience.

I remember more than once getting off at the side of the road in order to rest a few minutes. Then I would breathe a prayer, "O Lord, where are the men who ought to be riding these bicycles up and down these trails for you in Japan?"

As I made my visits and rounds on my bicycle I had to become accustomed to the sewage in the open ditches, the sharp stench and smells from the drains and from the intense fertilization of the country fields.

Another question often asked about our early days of Alliance work in Japan concerns the methods we used to reach the people. I would ride my bicycle to an area where there was a hotel or public lodging. I would rent a room for myself and then make up a poster and use it to announce that I would be holding a service. The service was not held in my own room but generally elsewhere in the lodging. There was a public space between two of the walls where people could come and sit on the floor. We began to reach a few people in this way, although it was slow work and called for patience.

Often I would meet the Japanese women, perhaps in the street, or perhaps at one of these services.

"May I call on you?" I would say to them, smiling my best smile.

But the national shyness and reserve based on their ancient traditions and customs caused them to reply, "Oh, we will come and see you!"

I knew that I was being put off but we had to live and abide by the traditions built up over the centuries.

Even later, when the women would become friendly enough to stop by my home and perhaps leave me a small gift of food, I would say, "Why don't you come in?"

Invariably, I would receive a shy smile and the answer, "I will come in some other time."

I also found that I had to observe this tradition myself when stopping by Japanese homes with a little gift of food. For the first several visits I would have to say, "Oh, I can't come in now, but I will some other time."

Perhaps after a half-dozen such exchanges of courtesy, I would feel that the time had come for me to accept the invitation to enter for a brief visit.

I remember the very first sermon that I tried to preach in Japanese. I had taken the Bible text, "Come to me, all you who are weary and burdened, and I will give you rest" (Matthew 11:28).

I found out after my message that I had used the wrong form of the verb. I had told them, "Come unto me . . . and I will give you *no* rest." A few of the boys in the group informed me of what I should have said and assured me that they understood what I meant!

The first message I actually gave was to a group of women in my own home. I told them about the coming of Christ and about the ministry of John the Baptist. I said to them, "He lived on locusts and secrets." You see, the Japanese words for "secrets" and "honey" are very much alike! Well, I was close!

Even before I became fluent in Japanese, I could tell very quickly whether the hearers were really taking in the Christian message. Some, hearing it for the first time, understood and were saved, while others took a long time.

Some just couldn't understand the plan of salvation. It is still that way today. It must be the working of the Holy Spirit. It is not the mental working—they can understand it with their heads—but it is when they get it in their hearts that the response begins.

Very few Japanese have a consciousness of being sinners before they hear the gospel. I think most of the repentance, the true repentance, among the Japanese, comes after they have accepted the True God and have opened their hearts to Him. Then they must see the beauty of Christ on display in our lives. I look back now and remember many things which spoke to me of my need to know Christ in the crucified life so that I wouldn't be a stumbling-block to the young Christians.

For instance, we had an elderly Japanese man in one of our groups who had been wonderfully saved. It was indeed a miracle. He would faithfully get up and give long testimonies, magnifying the Lord. But he had lost his teeth and he could not talk plainly. No one could understand him very well.

I used to sit there and pray, "O Lord, stop him. He is spoiling the meeting. Everything will go to pieces here."

One night the Lord spoke to me, "I can bless right over that old man. He is standing there trying to glorify me. But you do bother me by sitting here and fretting over it."

About 1930, we Christian missionaries in Japan had a great shaking up in our spiritual lives and in our attitudes toward the work of God and toward one another.

There was a young layman who had been brought into a deeper life through the original Oxford group (long before it became the Moral Re-Armament emphasis of today). He came out to Japan to give his testimony and he was wonderfully used of the Lord. Even with a missionary group, he did not use a theological approach. He simply said, "Listen to God. See what God will say to you!"

Well, when the missionaries began to listen to God, we had a time, I can assure you. There were humble confessions and getting right with one another and with God. It was remarkable.

As I had had a very deep experience with God, I said within myself, "Of course, this doesn't touch me." But it wasn't long before I found that it did touch me and that there were things I needed to consider. Again, the Lord began to show me different phases of the self-life I had not seen before.

It must be said that there was some trouble by people confessing things and situations in public where the confession should have been made either in secret or with one other person.

I remembered that in my early life, when I would get into a meeting where the Holy Spirit was working, I would be troubled by some of the things I had done. I never brought them out in a public meeting but there was a spiritual woman to whom I could go and the two of us took these things to the Lord. The things that were confessed never came up again.

I think there was much more need for instruction about those things, but at least we had a clearing in the whole missionary body. We learned a lot about sin and about the dealing of the Holy Spirit in those days. It was a preparation in revival and searching of our hearts for the hard days that were coming in the great war.

Now what about discouragement and disappointment in missionary life?

The Lord revealed to me in Japan, at a time when I was very discouraged, that I was created in answer to my mother's prayer for Japan and that the only business of my life was to spread the gospel in Japan.

You see, when I was so discouraged and the job seemed so terribly big, I thought, "Well, now, if I was married, I could follow my husband and there would be something doing. But what can one little person like me do?" I felt so hopeless!

And then the Lord said, "You are on the wrong track. I have a plan for your life and it is not for you to be married. I created you in answer to your mother's prayer."

Now, I don't know how to tell that! I heard it within my soul—I didn't hear it with these ears.

"Your only work in life," God continued, "is to spread the gospel among the Japanese; and if anyone should come and ask you to marry, he would be out of my will. Of this you can be sure— you needn't think anymore about it!"

Well, you know the whole thing passed out of my life like a cloud passing away and that was many years ago. The thought of marriage has meant nothing to me since that time—nothing!

9

Plain Words about the Self-Life

During the time that I was a student at Nyack Missionary Institute, I heard a guest missionary speaker make a statement in a chapel service that I found hard to believe at the time.

She said, "While you are in school and while you are at home, you are busy praying for souls. When you get to the mission field, you will find that you will be often praying for yourself."

I thought to myself, "She doesn't know very much about sanctification!"

After I had been in Japan for some time, I began to realize what the speaker had meant. I had had such wonderful experiences with God at home, wonderful experiences of seeing souls saved, and now everything seemed to shut down!

The worst of it was that every little while I saw an outcropping of self—my own desires, my own nature. I had supposed that "self" had been properly dealt with in my earlier experiences. I had been inclined to feel that Dr. Simpson wasn't quite up to the mark because he talked about the necessity of death to self and I thought he ought to talk about sanctification and the cleansing of the blood.

But on the field, the Lord said to me, "My method of dealing with the self-life is not cleansing—it is death!" And so God began dealing with me about this.

He spoke to me out of that passage in Philippians, "And being found in appearance as a man, he humbled himself and became obedient to death—even death on a cross" (2:8).

Through this the Spirit of God was saying to me, "You will have to go lower yet, if you will follow me!" I thought, "How can I go lower yet?" It seemed to me I was down to the last of everything and yet nothing seemed to pan out as I thought it should for a missionary.

I began searching and seeking the Lord with all my heart. I thought He would surely come down upon me with a wonderful anointing and baptism of the Spirit and that would be it! Then I would be able to go out and win souls.

But, on the contrary, He let one terrible experience after another come into my life and each time I would see some new form of the old life of self. When people talked against me, I was upset and wanted to justify myself. God dealt with me faithfully, step by step.

One morning, when I was back in the mountains, a missionary sang a hymn with the words, "I cannot live unless I die." God began to show me the secret of "Christ in you." I remember the morning He spoke to me about the fourth verse of the seventh chapter of Romans: "You also died . . . that you might belong to another."

Oh, how that expression came through to me— "married to another," married even to Him "who was raised from the dead in order that we might bear fruit to God."

I received such glorious assurance that He was bringing me into oneness with Himself. That's what marriage means—one with Christ, united with Him, and that all that He is, is mine.

I began to see that everything God allowed to come into my life had a purpose. If He allowed someone to be rude to me, the question was not about that person but about how I would take it and how would I react. God was always watching my reactions. From that time on, no matter how painful the lesson, if it shed some hitherto unknown light on the self-life, I could say, "O Lord, I am thankful to you for showing me this."

I remember how God used Andrew Murray's book about humility in my steps down.

"What is humility?" Andrew Murray asked. "Humility is never to be fretted, or vexed, or irritated, or sore, or disappointed." After reading that, I just threw the book down and wailed.

"Lord," I said, "I don't know anything about humility. I do get vexed. I get irritated. I get sore."

And then I read on, "It is to wonder at nothing that is done to me. It is to feel no resentment against anybody or anything. It is to be at rest when nobody praises me, when I am blamed or suspected. It is to have a blessed home in the Lord, where we can go in and shut the door, and kneel to our Father in secret, and be at peace in the deep sea of calm when all around is in trouble."

I could only breathe a prayer, "Lord Jesus, make that a reality in me. I must have it!"

And I thank Him because He has. It is a reality and it is just glorious.

But He had to take me down step by step, until one morning when I had been fasting and praying, His Word came to me, "If we are planted in the likeness of His death, we are in the likeness of His resurrection."

It seemed then like death was over and I was in the resurrection life. I knew full well what had taken place—God had brought me into oneness with His death. Not that there were not other things to learn, but I knew that even at the very core of my being He had brought me into oneness with His death and that He had actually taken over the full control of my life. "It is no more I, but Christ!"

How I rejoiced in Him. From that time on, life and ministry have been so different.

How true the words in Dr. Simpson's poem:

> Life's crisis had been past,
> And I had come at last
> Into the promised land of peace and rest.
> The crisis hour is o'er,
> And now forevermore
> I am dwelling in God's blessing and God's best.
>
> In time, I know not how,
> But this I know, that now

My life has found a new and nobler plane.
Something has passed away,
Something has come to stay,
And I can never be the same again.

The change is not in me;
Rather it seems that He
Has come Himself to live His life in mine;
And as I stepped aside
And took Him to abide,
He came and filled me with His life divine.

These things have become a glorious reality for
all of my days upon this earth under the teaching of
the Spirit of God. These are not the things you
learn out of a book. Troubles still come, but the
fretting and the soreness are no longer there.

At first, as I learned from Him, I would feel the
little things, but God said, "I will hold you right
there until you don't feel it anymore, because I
want you to be just as dead as Jesus was on the
cross."

So He just held me right on the gridiron until
there was no more feeling there. You see God does
not want us to be living in struggling and trying to
be like Christ, trying to do right, trying to be good.
He wants us to let the Good One come and dwell
within us. In order for that really to take place, we
have to subside: "I must decrease but He must in-
crease."

Let me testify that up to this very day, it has just
been one glorious life in Christ—all that He has is
mine! He is mine, and I am His forever. Our earth-

ly marriage covenant is until death separates. But
this one is forever and forever and forever. Death
doesn't have any effect on it—for I am His forever!

Another gracious experience came to me in
Japan at a time when I had been trying to extend
myself too far physically. I was sick and came to
the point of what we might call a nervous break-
down.

The Lord brought to my mind the life and ministry of Dr. Henry Wilson, one of the early associates
of A.B. Simpson. I could very clearly remember his
personal testimony of physical healing and the
presence of the Lord in his body day by day. Refer-
ring to his own time of sickness and physical need,
he told how he had found the meaning of
Zephaniah 3:17, "The Lord your God is with you,
he is mighty to save."

"He is my 'inside' God," Dr. Wilson said in his
testimony. "I am stronger at 70 than I was at 35."

So, in my physical need in Japan, the Lord
reminded me of Dr. Wilson's application of the
Scripture. In faith and simplicity I said to the Lord,
"You are what I need—I claim you as my 'inside'
God!" I saw that the Lord was something more
than the God in the midst of His people—He was
the living God, dwelling, healing within my own
being.

"Lord, I am going to trust you for your complete
work in every nerve center in my body, because you
have promised," I prayed earnestly.

God proved His faithfulness and every nerve was
healed and the condition was gone completely. For
all these years I haven't even known that I have any

nerves, because His resurrection life has been flowing through me. I guess I could say, like Dr. Wilson, "I am stronger in my 80s than I was many years ago, before I found the secret of the Lord, my 'inside' God!"

10

Genuine Conversions— Lasting Results

Much of my ministry throughout the years in Japan was related to the work of evangelism in the churches. At one time we could depend on street evangelism and meetings in public places, but there is too much traffic and too much noise now. We had to give that up because we were a nuisance and they were a nuisance. We had to recognize that the street belongs to the crowd, not to us.

Years ago we had only bicycles for evangelistic work. We traveled out into the country and would hire a room in a public hotel because they are always available. Then we would go out and call the people. Many would come. Almost invariably there would be some person interested who would stay and inquire, and often later would become the leader of the work in that section.

In my very early ministry as a young missionary, the first person to accept the Lord was a young banker, Mr. Nishida.

He came to a meeting where I was speaking and listened very intently. At the end of the service, he stayed and said, "My soul was so moved!" He became a Christian and began to help in the work immediately. He was later transferred to other areas, and if there was no Christian church when he arrived, he organized one before he left. You can still trace Mr. Nishida by the churches he organized, some in our work and some in the Nazarene denomination.

The second person to come to the Lord in Japan in my early ministry was a young girl from a very high-class family. After graduating from school, she came to me and said, "I am lonely now. I am through school and I don't know what to do. I want to know the meaning of life."

As I talked with her that day, she accepted Christ as her Savior. She lived with me and helped in the work for several years.

One of the next to be brought to Christ was Pastor Ogata, who worked with us so faithfully and with such leadership through the years. Considered to be a model young man among the Japanese, Mr. Ogata went into telegraph and post office work in 1920. After the death of his wife, he was transferred back to Fukuyama, the city in which I was located. He advanced very rapidly and was the youngest postmaster Japan ever had.

During a terrible flood, however, Mr. Ogata worked such long hours and strained himself so badly that he finally collapsed on the street. After an examination the doctor told him that three of

the vertebrae in his backbone were "just like jelly."
He was put into a cast. The doctors felt that there
was no hope for his recovery.

Mr. Ogata had never heard of God and knew
nothing of God. Two of the young men in the post
office became Christians at that time and they
wanted to get Mr. Ogata to the gospel services. By
holding him up under his arms and his shuffling
along in the cast, they got him to the church.

He picked up a Bible which we laid in front of
each place. It was opened to Timothy, where it says
there is one God and one mediator between God
and man—the man Christ Jesus.

He said to himself, "What a claim for these
people to make. Why, we have thousands of gods. I
would like to read this book." We didn't know who
he was, but we gave him permission to borrow the
book.

Soon there was a special meeting and the young
men brought him again. The evangelist preached
about the father of the prodigal son and the love of
the father.

As Mr. Ogata listened to the message and
recalled his love for his own children, he began to
weep at the thought that there was a God in
heaven who loved him like that. He wept until even
his garment was soaked with tears.

The young men who had helped him to the meeting took him home, but they said, "We could hardly
keep up with him!" He even forgot his cane because he was so happy about finding the Father in
heaven. He said to his second wife, "Oh, tonight I
met my heavenly Father!"

The wife thought to herself, "This is what the doctor said would happen. He has gone out of his mind!" She had never seen him with a smiling face before, as she had married him after he was taken ill.

The next morning when Mr. Ogata got up, he was walking around with a bright step, and she thought, "It certainly gives him strength to be out of his mind!" Mr. Ogata felt so well that he went to the barber shop. As he was telling the barber about finding his heavenly Father, he went over to the sink and stooped to wash his face.

Suddenly he thought, "Here I am stooping and it doesn't hurt me!" So Mr. Ogata went home and took off the cast. There was no pain at all!

He went to the doctor for an examination.

"What have you done to your body? That's not the same body you have been bringing in here!" the doctor exclaimed.

Mr. Ogata's body was completely healed. He did not know when it took place, but he was healed. So he notified the post office that he was all right and would be going back to work. Because they had already placed another man in his position, they said, "We will give you Hiroshima, the largest office in our section. We want you there."

Mr. Ogata was delighted. He wanted to make enough money for his family and to support students who could teach the gospel.

But God said to him, "I don't want your money and I will care for other students. I want *you* to go to school to prepare to preach."

Mr. Ogata's wife wouldn't agree to it and

reminded him of his responsibilities to his three daughters and the cost of getting them married.

But he answered, "I have to obey God before everything else."

So his wife said, "Why don't you go to school and obey God and I will take care of the children?" So Mr. Ogata went off to school.

Now, Japanese gentlemen in those days did not do menial work. But when Mr. Ogata went to school, he did kitchen work and even did the buying, which was very humbling for a gentleman. He really meant business for the Lord.

After some time, his wife came to me and said, "You know, I have been reading the Bible. It says, 'Come to me, all you who are weary and burdened, and I will give you rest' (Matthew 11:28). Now I was brought up in a Buddhist temple and my father was a priest there. But who would dare to say a thing like that—'Come . . . and I will give you rest'?" So I talked with her about Jesus and we knelt and prayed.

The next thing I knew, I heard she was up at the school with her husband and their girls were there with them. After completing Bible school, Mr. Ogata was sent to Matsuyama to work with me. He just stepped out, trusting God, for the salary of a preacher in those days was very, very small compared to that of the men in the post office.

Mr. Ogata lived close to the Lord. One day he told me that the Lord had spoken to him about a pattern for extending the Christian witness.

"God has given me a plan so that every year we should open one new station," he said. With the

Lord's help, year after year, we were able to open a new preaching station.

Through the years, Mr. Ogata became a leader of the Alliance work in Japan. Although he was a retiring man and not eager for position or election to office, he was a great spiritual influence in the church. At his death he had a glorious entrance into the presence of the Lord.

Another genuine conversion was that of Miss Mitsuko Ninomiya, a Japanese girl who is now our missionary to the Japanese in Brazil.

It was after the war when there was so much discouragement. Every morning I would go out on my bicycle to visit people and I would bow and smile.

Miss Ninomiya was one of the people I would greet each morning. Afterward she told me, "I would say to myself, 'Who can that be? How can anyone smile when we are in such a mess?' "

Finally, she said to a friend of hers, "Who is that woman who always smiles?"

"Don't you know?" the friend asked. "She is a missionary. She has been here a long time."

"A teacher of Christianity?" Miss Ninomiya exclaimed. She had always thought Christianity, that foreign religion, was the very last thing she wanted to hear about.

"Well, she is a very fine woman," her friend said. "Why don't you go to church with me today?" Because she was curious, Miss Ninomiya came.

Much to her surprise, when she got into the church, she found out I was the preacher.

She listened with great interest, but it took about a year before she really understood. But when she came to know the truth, she left everything for Christ. She had been a schoolteacher.

Miss Ninomiya felt the call of God to prepare and she came to our first little ragged postwar school. She was the first to graduate. The school was a little makeshift shack which made Dr. A.C. Snead, then the foreign secretary, shake his head when he saw it.

"This will never do!" he said with emphasis. But it did do for a time. It is wonderful just to be in this work with God. I wouldn't be anything but a missionary! What is all the wealth of the world? Nothing, compared with the joy of seeing God do things for mankind which no one else can do!

11

The Ministry Comes to Me

When public ministries were restricted by the Japanese before the war, my house in Matsuyama became a little hospital in miniature.

It had become so difficult to go out into public because I felt that, as an American, whenever I met someone, I stirred up animosity within them. I determined that to keep out of sight would be better, although I was still able to go out at that time.

A couple ladies who were sick needed a place to stay. One was a government official's wife who had tuberculosis and the other was one of our Christian women, the wife of a pastor. They came to my home and I took care of them.

There was also a young man who had been in our Bible school. He, too, was afflicted with tuberculosis. He had absolutely no one to take care of him. His own people were afraid of the disease and they didn't want him to come home.

He wrote to me and asked, "Can't I come to your house to stay? I am dying with TB."

I said, "Yes, you may come." He came at night because he knew how afraid everyone was.

When I talk about my house, some of you may be picturing the well-built, sturdy and efficient house you live in, in America. But my Japanese houses were not very good in comparison to that. I had moved many times and this last one was rather a poor place. In my earlier ministry, as a single lady, I had often lived with the Japanese instead of with an American companion.

Sitting on the mats on the floor with the Japanese was completely ordinary for me. I never really liked Japanese food, but I ate it, and it kept me going.

The Japanese used mats on the floor for sleeping, as well. For the most part, they would give me a room by myself, but it wasn't always possible because the homes were so small. I would like for you to have seen some of the places where I have slept!

In my own house, I did not have a bed at first. In Fukuyama, I didn't have a bed for years. For dining, I used a little, low Japanese table. I wouldn't advise other missionaries to do that, but I did it. I am sure my body suffered. I did not have a stove but only the charcoal fire. I often sat with my overcoat on. It was too heavy, so my shoulders became terribly painful from the weight.

My brother Tom, also a missionary in Japan, found it very hard to sit on the floor, Japanese style, for long periods of time. His long legs would get cramped and "go to sleep." So he had a square box made and had it painted black. He always strapped it to his bicycle when he started out to visit and kept his papers and tracts and Bible inside.

In the late 30s, with the Japanese military really bristling, Tom would get so frustrated making his visits. Often he was stopped by an officer or policeman or agent because he would take the black box into a home. They would demand, "What do you have in that box?" He would have to open the box for inspection.

Tom went back to the States for furlough, and my sister Anne and I stayed on. After the war broke out, we heard nothing from Tom. Because of his superior knowledge of the Japanese language, the United States government wanted him to work actively in the intelligence against the Japanese.

"No," Tom said, "I learned this language to save the Japanese, to help them to know God, and I can't use it to help fight against them."

The government finally asked him to be the chaplain in a factory where materials were being made for the armed forces.

"Well," he said, "I can do that. I can tell men about the gospel."

One day, one of the men at the factory became a Christian. Tom went home exceedingly happy. It was that very same night that he was stricken with a heart attack and went to be with the Lord.

Throughout all of this time of suspicion before the war, Anne and I were separated. The authorities would not allow either of us to cross the inland sea so we could meet.

As I was praying one day, there came to my mind a vision of a couple of men holding back their dogs on a leash, with the dogs just tearing to get at each other.

The Lord said to me, "I hold this whole situation. It won't break until I get ready for it to break. I hold both sides, so you don't need to worry, for when I let it come, I'll have you on my mind. I will take care of you!"

Anne and I had decided by that time, that whatever came, God wanted us to stay. Our hearts were set to remain.

12

Enemy Nationals

Miss Akiko Koizumi, a Japanese girl who had lived with me and worked for me for seven years in Matsuyama, rushed into the house. "Sensei! It's come; it's come!"

I didn't realize what she meant, on that December morning in 1941, or why she was so upset.

"The war, Sensei, the war! It has broken out," she blurted.

"Oh, it can't be," I told her.

"Yes, it is true; it has broken out," she almost screamed.

This was how I found out about the start of the war.

There had been so little about the coming war that we could say to one another. I knew it was foolish and so did my friends, but I could tell what was in the mind of my Japanese friends and the Christians who were nearby—they were wondering what would happen to me.

And I, of course, was wondering what would happen to Anne. I did not have any way of knowing it for some time, but just three hours after the declaration of war was broadcast, the police arrived at my sister's house in Fukuyama. They allowed her only a few minutes to pack some bedding, clothing and a few kettles, and then they marched her off to the police station.

She spent three days at the police headquarters, always wondering if I were going through the same experience. Then she was escorted by four policemen and turned over to the officers in charge of the prison camp at Miyoshi.

The word that Anne was going to be transferred from the Fukuyama police headquarters to the mountain prison camp at Miyoshi spread quickly to all of the churches. All along the line, groups of Christian believers boarded the train at their own station and rode to the next station, hoping to give a little comfort along the way.

The police proved their kindness because they refrained from putting the customary basket over the prisoner's head. Anne was able to see those who felt so deeply for her, although she could not speak with them. An Englishman, two English teachers, a drug addict, a priest and 11 nuns became her companions in prison at Miyoshi.

I had no idea how she would be treated, but as I prayed about it, God gave me great peace about the way in which He would care for her.

Actually, as it turned out, the Japanese officer in charge of the Miyoshi prison was a very kind man. There were rules and regulations, naturally, and one of them was that Anne was not supposed to write to anyone on the outside. This officer, however, allowed her to write to me and he personally took her letters out and mailed them.

Not only that, but he allowed the letters which I continued to write to be sent in to her and as the head of the camp he also informed me that I would be allowed to send her any food that I could get.

The police also came to my home in Matsuyama on the day after the war started. I believe my friends expected that I would be taken away immediately. Personally, I didn't know what to expect.

"Do you realize that you are now classified as an enemy national?" the police asked me.

"Yes," I told them, but I assured them that I had no intention of doing anything harmful, that I realized I was still a guest in Japan.

They asked me to sign the official papers that I recognized myself to be an enemy national and that I would not do anything contrary or in hindrance to their plans for the war against the United States. They said I would not be put in an internment camp immediately, but that I could stay in my own house under guard.

The police gave me a little book and I had to write down the name of anyone who came to my home. Every time I went out I had to tell where I was going. That's all the agreement there was at that time. I think it was fair in time of war.

I lived that year just like I had before—the Lord took care of me. The girl with me, Akiko Koizumi, was a wonderful example of love and devotion, although she was suspected of collaboration and was warned to leave my home. She brought in many of our daily needs of food.

There was also a teacher who felt he wanted to

help me. He not only obtained garden produce for me, but chickens as well. He also brought what they call "miso"—a fermented bean soup which is very nourishing. The government did not care if people came and brought food—they just didn't want interference nor talk against their plans.

One policeman had his mind made up to use me to get a promotion, so he informed the authorities that Pastor Ogata was telling me things about the war that were not suitable for me to know. The other policeman, who was taking such good care of me, saw that I was troubled and I told him what I had heard.

He talked with Mr. Ogata who confirmed that we had not talked about the government. "Well, you tell her not to be anxious. I'll just take care of that!" he told Mr. Ogata. Since he had the superior position, he went to the younger officer and told him everything was checked out and there was nothing to it. As far as I knew nothing further came of the incident.

During the year that I was under house arrest, as I thought of the devotion and prayers of Japanese friends, I reviewed the contrast to my earliest days in Japan.

Loving the Japanese people as I did when I arrived in 1909, it was hard for me to realize that they were afraid of me as a foreigner in those early years. The people were told over and over that we were spies. The leaders would caution them, "Don't trust these foreigners. No one is really that altruistic. They have some other motive and must be connected with their government." The blessed thing was that we never heard this sentiment expressed after World War II.

In those days of distrust, the people were often reminded by leaders and politicians that "this Christian religion doesn't agree with our national religion." Japanese teachers were forbidden to hear the Christian gospel lest it should get into the public life through the schools.

We found, however, that the people really wanted to listen and, deep down in their beings, would consider the truth. But I did hear them warned more than once to wait, that the gospel must be too good to be true.

Even the contacts with the children had been hard to make. We gave a little talk, using a magnet to show how the nails were picked up by the magnet, as an object lesson of the love of God bringing us to the Savior. But the children, in trying to repeat the story to their parents, brought wrath upon us all, for the parents said, "Nails, nails! That's it! Those are the nails that they will use to hang you on the Christian cross!" Such was the strength of the traditional Shinto religion in the hearts and minds of the people of Japan in those days.

One could not help having an ache in your heart for the groping Japanese people. Millions of them worshiped all kinds of idols, their temples and shrines virtually littering the land.

Japan has always desired to have recognition for unparalleled material advancement, but many other things in their culture and daily life called for prayer and compassion on the part of those who had met Christ.

What would you say of a father who goes to a temple, tosses a coin into a box and rings a bell to wake up the bronze Buddha before him, in order to ask if it is safe to buy this or sell that?

What would you say of a mother who ties a cloth bib around the neck of a stone image to cure her child's cold or to take care of the spirit of a child who has died?

What would you say of a nation which, in the past, expected its war heroes to gather at Patriot's Shrine and there give thanks to their ancestors for Japan's success, because ancestral worship was a dominant force for centuries?

What would you say of a moral philosophy that, for so long in the nation's culture, legalized and licensed the Yoshiwara, the district of prostitution, in metropolitan Tokyo? To the traveler, the Yoshiwara was Tokyo's most astonishing feature, for several thousand girls were kept for three years each, none being allowed to leave the quarter without a permit during her term of servitude. Men who visited Tokyo had reason to write home and say, "It is one of the sights of Japan to wander through these streets and see the hundreds of girls on exhibition behind wooden bars, like tigers in ornate cages."

Small wonder that God laid upon the hearts of faithful missionaries the need of the saving, healing power of Jesus Christ in Japan!

13

"Tomorrow"

I was busy taking care of the three sick people in my home. Although I was under a police guard, almost a year went by after the Pearl Harbor attack before three policemen came to the door and said, "Tomorrow you will be taking the train to Yokohama." They didn't tell me why, but I learned later that a group of Americans were to be exchanged for Japanese prisoners in the United States.

I asked what they planned to do about the sick people in my house.

"We will take care of them," they promised. "They will go to the hospital if necessary."

It seemed that the Holy Spirit whispered to me, "Don't say a word. You must do as you are told."

The policemen took the young man with tuberculosis and placed him in a Red Cross hospital. He died there a few days later.

Christian friends and neighbors prepared a final meal for me as a farewell gesture and we had a blessed time even though we had that "going away" feeling. I gave away most of my belongings to the Christian friends.

When my "tomorrow" came and it was time to take the train, I said to the police, "I am not going without some word from my sister." They knew, of course, that Anne was also to be one of the group included in the exchange, so they said, "She will be with you." Then the policeman who was to take me to the railroad station said to me, "I know that in the community it is a disgrace to be seen walking with a policeman. Therefore I will go ahead and you can walk behind me."

All of my Japanese friends knew what was happening and they felt sorry that I should be there under these conditions of war and compulsion. Some stood along the street weeping as I passed by. Others lined up by the side of their houses and with little sign of outward emotion signaled with an almost imperceptible flutter of their fingers that they recognized me and were adding their own farewell.

You can imagine what all of this meant to me—the respect and friendship and regard of my Japanese neighbors at a time when I was considered a prisoner and an enemy national by the officials. These gestures were particularly significant because during those war years the feelings and emotions of the people had been whipped up by the propagandists until they didn't know what to believe. Day after day they were told many awful things, things that would upset anybody.

The pastor in Matsuyama and some of the Christian believers asked if they could accompany me on the train. Permission was given. One would never have known that I was a prisoner, from anything that was done there, but when we got to Yokohama

I realized that I was not free anymore.

I looked out the window of the room they gave me in Yokohama. I could see some ships. One had several large white crosses painted on its side. After several days, workmen began painting over the white crosses. The exchange deal was off.

I learned later that when the American officials had been approached about the exchange in which the Japanese wanted to send back all who were Americans, they said, "Nothing doing, if you are sending deportees. If they wish to come, that's something else." Of course, we were all deportees who had made up our minds to stay in Japan.

From my hotel room in Yokohama I was taken to a camp in Tokyo in a Black Mariah. In America they are called paddy wagons. Well, they brought these two black vans and put the whole bunch of us in.

In Tokyo, I was first interned in a hotel. There were other Americans there also, most of them teachers or missionaries. Then we were transferred to a large house which had been part of a Catholic orphanage. We were examined and questioned again.

I remember an experience I had at this point because all of my belongings were in one trunk and it was too heavy for me to carry to the room to which I was assigned. I said to a Japanese policeman, "Who can I get to help me with my trunk?" He turned to me and said with sarcasm, "Who do you think you are? You are just an enemy national. Carry your own trunk!"

Within my own heart I thought, "Is this all that I get from the Japanese people after all these years of service and ministry?"

I remember it didn't take the Lord Jesus very long to examine my heart, and the Spirit of God said to me, "Is that what you have been doing in Japan all these years? Have you actually been serving and ministering so that you should be appreciated?"

Well, when the Lord spoke to me that way, everything that was considered hardship or difficulty or trial went to the cross, and I said, "Dear Lord, forgive me! I really have not been here to be appreciated. I have been here to witness to your love!"

And insofar as the trunk was concerned, some of the other ladies who were being interned with me helped me and we got it to the right place.

Within a few weeks, the camp in which my sister was being held was broken up. When she was told that she was being taken to Tokyo, one of the supervisory policemen happened to be a person she had known when he was a little boy. Something decent came through in his character, too, as he quietly said to her, "You should be happy because you are going to see your sister today."

Late in the day, looking down from a window, I saw the arrival of this group. I cannot tell you how my heart reacted when I saw Anne getting out of the vehicle with the other internees.

Even as she stood in the yard, waiting for the next order, I could sense that she was affected by all of the things she had passed through during the many long months that we had been separated. Finally, she was in the building and we were face to face.

"Oh, Andy!" I cried out, my girlhood name for her rushing to my lips in the joy and emotion of our reunion.

The quarters were so crowded that there was no privacy for us in that precious moment, so I guided her to a back stairway at the rear of our floor. There was nobody there, and it was a good thing, for I am sure we were just like two young girls, hardly believing it possible that we were going to be together for the reminder of the war at least.

Actually, the war camp experiences had crushed Anne in many ways, and after she came to Tokyo there were still many trials to bear.

First of all, there was really no place for her on our floor—all of the available spaces were already taken. She had to lie on the floor in front of the doorway and throughout the night there were those who had to come and go. All of them had to step right over her head.

But what a comfort it was for us to be together again. You really can't know what it means until you have been in such a circumstance. Now we were able to share, to pray and study together. The Lord had brought her to me and it was my privilege to be her encouragement for the hard times that followed.

My audiences know that I haven't used our wartime experiences in Japan to draw out sympathy either for my sister or for myself. I was thankful every day and every hour that she had been allowed to come to Tokyo to be with me for the duration. There were things I could do for her and I also had the satisfaction of knowing that even though we were not comfortable, at least we were together and we could talk together and pray and encourage one another.

14

"Give Us Our Daily Bread"

We were ultimately moved to a large building which seemed to be part of a Catholic monastery which the Japanese had taken over. When we were first taken to Tokyo, our group of ladies consisted of more than 90 sisters and nuns and between 60 and 70 Protestant missionaries and teachers.

After getting to Tokyo, there was one more opportunity for repatriation on the steamship *Gripsholm*. Most of the Catholic sisters decided to take advantage of the opportunity to go home. Quite a few of the Protestant women did as well.

The police came to us at that time and said, "We think you had better go. We can't promise what may happen." But those of us who had made up our minds previously told them that we felt it was the will of God for us to stay. Our group finally consisted of about 30 Protestant missionaries and probably almost that many Catholic nuns from two different orders.

There were lonely days. We knew in our hearts

that the last opportunity to leave the island was past, but we committed ourselves to the Lord and felt great peace in the midst of our circumstances.

In the first stages of our detention in the internment camps, the conditions weren't so bad. We had food regularly, and also a cook.

Because the Swiss were neutral in the war, a Swiss monk was put in charge of our welfare. Occasionally he would bring a couple cans of jam or some other item of food from the American embassy. So we would each have a spoonful of jam. That is quite a treat, you know, when you are really hungry!

We were allowed to have books to read. These also were brought from the American embassy. I believe they belonged to the ambassador. They would bring a bundle of books, take them back, and then bring others. I read histories of America and a biography of Abraham Lincoln during that time.

We were also allowed to study in groups. Some French nuns taught us French. I thought it would be better for my mind to study French than to go on in Japanese, because I had grooves where the Japanese language ran. The French was something new and challenging. It kept me bright.

I was much more thick-skinned than my sister. Because she had such a sensitive nature, everything the police did bothered her.

Among the Japanese over us in the camp was a loud and foolish boy who was retarded. He served as an errand boy for the police. My sister worried about him because he was so unpredictable. He had a temper and Anne was afraid of him.

It was very hard to get any kind of warm water, to

say nothing of hot water, for washing our clothes. One morning one of the nuns got a tub of warm water and she had her clothes in the tub. This ill-tempered boy came along and, because he wanted to wash his trousers, he just emptied the tub and took it away.

The sister responded sweetly, "Let me have your trousers and I will wash them for you." She was a real saint. I loved that dear old lady. She was one of those they called the "working nuns" as compared to the "teaching nuns."

As the months went by, our food in the camp became worse and worse. We heard that the Japanese government had made provision for food for our class of prisoners, so we began to wonder why we had so little food and why it was so bad.

Finally it became known that our camp cook sold much of the good food and pocketed the profits. As a result, we were getting meat rations consisting of porpoise or shark or whale meat, and even these provisions became more and more scarce. We really learned to pray, "Give us this day our daily bread." We didn't say it—we prayed it.

It was the law that each internee be given one pound of bread each day. Two little buns make a pound. At first we had nice bread, but it also became worse and worse because there was no flour. Ultimately our bread flour was made of peanut shells and corn cobs finely ground.

We would have those two buns in the morning. Then at noon we were supposed to get a cup of thin rice. If we ate all of that at noon, there was nothing at night, for that was the ration of food for the day. So we found we had to try to save something at noon to eat in the evening or we would be too hungry to sleep at night.

Did you ever try to eat soy beans? Well, try it some time. Try cooking them. You can cook them for five hours and they will be just as hard as when you started. We had soy beans. When they gave them to us whole we couldn't eat them. But every three days they ground them and made a soup. That would go down.

Then the International Red Cross sent in some boxes. These contained corned beef and powdered milk, sugar, raisins, a can of some kind of fruit. I learned that after I had eaten some of the good Red Cross food, my stomach would accept some of the more repulsive items again for a while. Three times we had distribution of Red Cross boxes and that's what kept us alive. The very fact that these Red Cross boxes were delivered to us in the camp, when the Japanese people were in such straits for food themselves, speaks well for the men who were in charge of the camp and for all who handled the shipments along the way.

I remember well the day when the police came in and said, "No bread today—we just don't have any!" That day we looked to the Lord and prayed, "All right, Lord, if you want us to go without bread today, it is all right with us."

That very day a Japanese lady in the area had taken her spinach out of the ground in order to plant something else. She came to the camp with a big basket of the spinach sprouts and said to the leader, "I don't think those ladies have too much of anything like this. Perhaps they would be glad for this spinach." So we had spinach. Oh, wasn't it good!

I don't think there was ever a day when we had absolutely nothing. Sometimes we were out of salt. We found out that one can get along without sugar much better than without salt. At that time, they finally brought in a big chunk of dirty, hard salt. It was the kind of chunk they set out and let the cows lick in the fields. It didn't make any difference to us how dirty it was—it was salt!

It wouldn't be right to tell about these conditions in our camp without putting in a word about the Japanese man who was chosen by the authorities to be in charge of the internees. I am sure that when he was given this responsibility he was told to mistreat us because we were a part of the enemy.

But he never did. Actually he was a good and considerate man. I wouldn't even mind giving him the title of a noble man, because after the end of the war he became a Christian and a deacon in one of the Protestant congregations in Tokyo.

As internees, we were each allowed to have some funds with us. Even though this man over us was stiff in his position of leadership, and sometimes curt and brusque, we would give him money and he would go out and buy vegetables for us from the farmers. We were not allowed to go out, so we appreciated him purchasing the produce for us.

After the war he told us, "I saw that you people had something that I didn't know anything about." He didn't mean American humanitarianism—but the love of Christ shed abroad in our hearts so that we could love those who were really our enemies.

15

The Emperor Ends the War

Toward the end of the war in August 1945, as the bombings increased, there were fires all around us in the city every night. While we did not have any actual contact with the outside, we could hear the B-29s. In our hearts we knew that it was only a matter of time.

Finally, about the same time that the Emperor's palace was bombed and burned, our camp was destroyed. There was no place to put us. The bomb did not actually strike our building, but Waseda University was nearby and, when it burned, the flames blew over onto our building.

The guards told all of us to hurry down the steps, out the back door, and to wait together at a certain place on the next street. We all went down there and sat down on some stones until someone came along and said, "You know, there's a time bomb right over there in back of you!"

We moved pretty quickly, I can assure you.

There in the street we watched the last of our belongings go up in flames. Many things pass through your mind as you see what little you have left being destroyed.

The police and guards arrived and told us to start walking. There were fires all around us. Apparently there was no plan set up for such an emergency, so we just continued walking, walking until daylight came.

We saw many sad sights on that night walk through the bombed and burning streets—a poor mother, discouraged, distressed, the father killed, the children whimpering at her side. Where should they go? They no longer had a home. It was a terrible sight—enough to make us forget about ourselves.

At last they directed us to an empty old school building. They brought us some hardtack and heated water and gave us something to drink. We were there all day.

I wanted to wash my face. A man saw me trying to wash in a fish bowl. He said, "Come over here, lady, and I will show you a place to wash." He took me just outside the gate to a little pond in his yard.

The police came running after us, shouting, "Don't you know she can't get out?" They pulled me back inside. But I got my face washed anyhow.

That night we were taken to the Franciscan hospital. We were all put in a room usually oc- cupied by the novices in the order. The thing I remember about that place, more than anything else, is the mosquitoes. If you really want to suffer, just go to Japan without a mosquito net!

With these events in Tokyo, we knew that the war was just about over. It was only a few days later that the Emperor made the public pronouncement of surrender.

The history books are full of the details of the surrender, but I only want to remind you about the attitude of Emperor Hirohito himself. He finally realized how long he had been duped and deceived by some of his military and government advisers. When the imperial palace was bombed and burned, these men gave out a report that the "palace was slightly damaged."

"Slightly damaged!" the Emperor exclaimed. "Why, it is completely gone!"

Through that his eyes were opened.

"They have deceived me," he said. "They have not been fair with me."

Some of those leaders still begged him not to surrender the nation and to allow a great military stand against American invaders on the beaches of the home islands. They actually crawled on their hands and knees and took hold of the Emperor's coat, begging him. But he turned his back and said, "I am not willing that my people should suffer anymore."

The top general and others went out and committed suicide in the yard.

When the Emperor made his announcement by radio, the people were shaken and choked with emotion. For one thing, they had never heard the voice of their Emperor before. For another, many had the idea that the Emperor might command all of the Japanese to commit suicide rather than fall into the enemy's hands.

We listened with the nurses and others in the hospital where we were quartered. There was great tenderness in the voice of the Emperor, his voice almost breaking with emotion. He announced that the war was over because he felt the people of Japan had endured enough suffering. I don't think there could have been a dry eye in Japan as the announcement was made.

You can imagine what happened inside the minds and hearts of the Japanese people. Some actually dropped dead. Others fell in the street and went into an exhausted sleep when the Emperor said, "The war is over!"

We were told to go back to our rooms and that we would be informed later how our actual release would come about. Actually we were still in the interment camp two weeks after the end of the war because there was no other place to go. You can hardly imagine what the housing situation was like in battered Tokyo. It was even worse in some other cities. There were no vehicles for transportation and there was no system for communicating with those on the outside.

The American planes began to drop provisions, however, because they knew that prisoners of war, internees and even many of the Japanese people themselves were starving. They dropped supplies around our camp, but they didn't have the proper parachutes so many of the cases of food popped when they struck the ground. We found one whole case of stewed fruit and every can had been broken open. The juice was gone, but we gave the pieces of fruit to the sick people in the hospital. We shared sugar and everything that was dropped for us.

I can laugh now about one instance, but it was not humorous at the time. The airmen dropped cases of men's clothing and men's shoes for the GI prisoners of war. After we got all the bags open and all of the clothing for the men laid out, our Japanese camp leader selected a suit that fit him and put it on. He then came around to our rooms, saluted us, and said, "My dear ladies, you are now free!" We couldn't get the clothes to Americans, so we distributed them to the Japanese who were in such need.

We now had no Mission board to back us and no one to whom we could appeal but to God. God gave me the promise in Second Chronicles 16:9: "For the eyes of the LORD range throughout the earth to strengthen those whose hearts are fully committed to him."

"The eyes of the LORD. . . ." He knew where the money was and where our help would come from. He was to be our Source of strength all through those days, as one miracle followed another.

Interlude

Soon after occupying Japan in 1945, General MacArthur said to his aides in Tokyo, "Let's get the missionaries back into Japan. There is a vacuum here that only the missionaries can fill."

Most missionaries were on distant shores. But two bright-faced, smiling and eager American women were in Tokyo—Mabel Francis and Anne Dievendorf—just coming out of the wartime camp to survey the great needs of the Japanese people.

"We are only two," they said to one another, "and Tokyo is a city of seven million people. Where will we start?"

They didn't have to wonder very long. An American soldier in the occupation forces and his Christian buddies were on a crowded train in Tokyo. They saw an American woman, but it wasn't until she smiled that the light dawned.

"She's got to be an American missionary," the leader of the GI group said.

So when Mrs. Dievendorf pushed her way out of the train, the American soldiers were right behind her.

"Are you a missionary?" they asked. She told them who she was. "We didn't know how to get hold of an American missionary, but we are looking for a place where we can meet and go right on with our gospel hour which we started in the Philippines," they told her.

She took the young men to the Japanese pastor of the First Methodist Church, located on the main street of Tokyo. He was delighted at the idea. The church had a big hole in the roof from a bomb, but the GIs were glad for the hole in the roof because the happy singing sounded out all over the center of that war-sick city.

The lives of thousands of frustrated Japanese people were affected by these groups of American soldiers who sang and preached and prayed and witnessed and helped during every spare moment away from their regular duties with the occupation forces. Many who crowded into that bombed-out Methodist church night after night could not understand English, but they understood the Christian satisfaction in those young faces and the earnestness of their proclamation of grace and love through Jesus Christ. Hundreds came forward to find peace with God.

At the center of all this—interpreting, guiding, assisting, calling, distributing clothing and food to the needy of Tokyo—were the bright, happy American missionary women. God had given them an immediate ministry in Tokyo.

Mabel Francis kept writing to Dr. A.C. Snead, the foreign secretary of The Christian and Missionary Alliance in New York, reminding him of the great opportunity for Christ in post-war Japan. Finally she said, "If the Alliance really is not coming back to work in Japan, then tell us with which evangelical group we should join forces. I have not been in America for 26 years, so I do not know the church situation. We don't want to be independent. Our churches need the leadership and fellowship of the Alliance."

Some time later the answer came: "The Alliance is coming back into Japan and the Rev. Paul McGarvey has been chosen as the board's representative."

Mabel Francis recalls, "We were delighted and we stood with open arms to receive him. It was a great joy to be able to throw the burden, which I didn't know how to carry, over on him. Mr. McGarvey has done a wonderful work. He has the respect and honor of the whole missionary group in Japan."

16

America's Failure in Japan

Anyone who was not in Japan after the surrender to the Allies in 1945, cannot imagine the confusion, the hopelessness, the despair, the rubble and the restrictions because so many things were in ruins.

Wherever you went in Tokyo, you had to make your way around ruined buildings, piles of rubble, abandoned trucks and vehicles that had been bombed and burned. This put a most unusual strain on the trains. Every trip was jammed because it was the only transportation available. The aisles would be so full that people couldn't get in. But they would come anyway—right through the window onto your lap! The doors just couldn't handle the crowds.

Anne and I knew that it would be months before we would be able to get the necessary transportation to go to our old homes and visit the Christians who still might be alive at Matsuyama, Hiroshima, Fukuyama and other cities where there had been churches before the war. You can imagine what a test of patience it was to wonder how the Christian friends and the churches had fared during the long months of war and the bombings, and, of course, the use of atomic weapons.

But there was no way to get any word. We worked in the Tokyo area for several months with those American soldiers who were in the occupation forces but who were carrying on a Christian ministry in their spare hours. There must have been about 400 of these boys leading gospel services. The GIs were busy bringing in any of their companions who were willing to come, but the Japanese people began to find out that they, too, were welcome to attend. They did not go near army installations, but there was no one to forbid them from coming to the gospel services. They crowded in until they nearly crowded us out.

The amazing thing was that the Japanese didn't understand what these boys were saying. They would give their testimonies in English, with shining faces, as the Spirit of God worked. When the invitation was given, the Japanese would come forward, filling the altars.

The GI boys had gotten Japanese Testaments and marked appropriate passages which they could point out to the seekers. Many of the boys learned to read some of these passages in Japanese.

Anne and I were kept busy interpreting in these services. We couldn't reach all the Japanese who came, for there were so many, but the boys would get to them and we would find people shouting "hallelujah" because the Lord had met them.

There will be many in heaven as a result of those

days. We were so thankful for this ministry because we were at least a little help in such a great sea of need.

In those days of tension in Tokyo, not all Americans were doing good. But although American soldiers were involved in many other things in the unwholesome areas, the Japanese were amazed that the occupying forces were so kind and so willing to help the Japanese. There were many stories of their tender dealings with the populace.

One woman told me, "You know, we thought that when these American soldiers came in that all of the women would be molested and that we would have a terrible time. So in our neighborhood we strung up a system of bells. If anyone was molested, she would ring the bells and we would all come and get the culprit and kill him.

"But we didn't need to feel like that," she continued. "They have been so kind. The other day I was coming home from the market with my vegetables loaded on my back. I could hardly stand on the tram because of my load. I couldn't reach the strap. One of those big soldiers came in and pulled a Japanese man off the seat and said to me, 'Sit down!' I was so thankful."

The American chaplains were also a great force for good during those days. We would go to places to visit and would find a mother weeping and saying, "What will I give my children to eat tonight?"

Often the chaplains would get army rations that were being thrown away. The chaplains would get a jeep and collect these cans and bring them out to

us. We would distribute the food to those in need.
It was a day of privilege. People were glad to get
old beans or dirty sugar or anything else they could
eat.

General MacArthur did everything he could to
raise the standard of living. If no one else could get
to him, he always had time to listen to the women
of Japan. He gave them preference and he gave
them the right to vote. He lifted their status a great
deal. World War II brought some good side effects
for the women of Japan.

During the first 10 years after the war, the
Japanese people were very open and seeking. Our
churches in America, however, did not grasp the
opportunity—they didn't send a thousand missionaries! History records what has happened in
the years since the war.

17

Survivors

The winter months passed and it was February 1946 before Anne and I could get down to Matsuyama. Tight restrictions on transportation, building materials and other aspects of the Japanese economy were still in effect.

Matsuyama was terribly damaged, much like Hiroshima, but the ruins came from repeated bombings over a longer period, while in Hiroshima, the whole city was demolished in one flash of light. Only one house was left standing in the entire neighborhood where I had lived.

A most amazing thing happened when I met the lady who lived there. I learned that the government had instructed the people to paste strips of heavy paper over the seams and windows so the concussions which resulted from the bombing would not do as much damage.

The lady of the house said to herself, "If I am to paste strips of paper on the inside, I'm going to have them mean something." She pasted Japanese characters over her window which said, "The battle is not yours, but God's."

In another place she had put, "Ye shall not need to fight in this battle," and again, "The Lord your God, He it is that fights for you."

We learned that she had an upstairs room which she rented out, but when we talked to her in March, the room was occupied. She later wrote us and said, "I now have a vacant room. If you wish to come, I would love to have you at my house."

So, with God's provision in that single house, we went down to Matsuyama. The room was only 9 feet by 12 feet, but we lived there for four years. The only furniture we had was a bed. There wasn't room for a table or any other furniture. We sat on the floor. We even ate on the floor. Everything was done in real Japanese fashion.

All the time we had been in Tokyo, we were trying to collect things to take back to our people in Matsuyama. We knew the Christians would be destitute, both there and in all parts of Japan.

My home was gone. My sister's home was gone. Not one church building was left standing in any of the cities. Everything was gone!

What could we do? There simply was no material for building any kind of structure, either a home or church. There was nothing to be purchased anywhere.

I remembered that I had read an account of a doctor in China who had "prayed up" the walls of a hospital. I thought, "If he could pray up the walls of a hospital in China, we certainly can pray up the walls of a church!" And that's how we began to pray that God would provide us with materials for a church building.

Anne and I heard that one of the American contingency military units would be moving out soon. We immediately made plans to call on the colonel in charge of the base.

By this time we had found the pastor who had been in charge of the church in Matsuyama and a few of the Christians. We told them that probably some things would be thrown away at the base as the unit prepared to move on.

Our visit revealed that it was a military police unit moving out. That cooled our enthusiasm a bit, but I reminded Anne that faint hearts never won anything. So we rapped on the door of the outer office at the base. A big, burly Irishman came to the door. He had such blue eyes and he looked us over from head to foot.

"Well, girls, where did you come from?" he said, inviting us in.

We had the chance to tell about our missionary work and the needs of the people and the churches and that we hoped they might have some things to discard.

"We would be glad for even a board," I told him.

He thought for a few moments, and then said, "Well, there is a house down on the airfield which has been condemned by the army, and they are going to pull it off into the sea. There's a lot of good material in that house. Would you like to go down and take a look at it?"

He put us into a jeep and we started off.

Now, in those postwar days, it was against the rules for an American to transport females, for there were only Japanese girls. A military unit saw us driving along in the jeep and drove in front of us and stopped. These men were going to scold the driver of the jeep.

And then they saw Anne and me—two elderly American women.

"Say, where did you get 'em?" they shouted at our driver.

There was a lot of material, including electric wiring, which you couldn't buy anywhere in Japan at that time. The building was made of corrugated iron. There was a big table of thick plywood, which was also unobtainable in Japan. We told him we could use practically everything that was there.

The colonel said, "There is one stipulation— everything is to be off the base in three days. That's our deadline for having the site cleared up when we leave."

We told him we didn't have even a hammer.

"All right, we'll loan you hammers," he said.

We found one Japanese boy who was not working, so Anne and I and that boy worked all day with those heavy claw hammers. We loosened great strips of corrugated iron and laid them together on the ground.

Once in a while Anne and I would stop and look at each other and say, "How are we ever going to carry all this into the city?" There was no such thing as hiring a truck then. All of the Japanese trucks had been destroyed.

But we would turn back to our work with a prayer, "Lord, you know all about this. You know this material has to be carried up to the city somehow."

Toward evening a big American army truck pulled up to the site. The driver said the colonel was worrying about how we ladies were going to get the materials from the base into the city. The truck was there to help us.

By that time we had gotten down to the framework of the building and had only a few of the higher pieces taken off. Well, the driver hitched the truck right onto that frame and pulled the whole thing down at once.

You have probably never seen any women happier than we were then!

Some of the American boys loaded the sheet iron and the lumber framework. We never could have done it. They drove the truck into the city to the property where the church was to be built.

One of our Japanese young men who held some kind of position in the provincial government offices told us of another group of buildings that was to be disposed of on an American base.

Anne and I again went to the base offices to get more information. This colonel, however, was of a different nature. He told us the Americans were not in Japan to build churches—and that was that!

But the Christian young man urged us to try again. He didn't want to give up. Reluctantly, we went to the base and asked to see the colonel once more. We were told he had just been transferred. So we were escorted into the presence of his successor.

"Of course you ought to have one of those buildings," he said. "But these decisions have to be referred to the governor of the precinct be-

cause we want the approval and cooperation of
the Japanese officials."

The kind of petition which we had to have, to
present to the governor, sounded very complicated.
But our young layman assured us that he could
write the proper language. And so the document
was prepared. We took it to the governor's office.

After we had presented our petition, the governor
said, "I have a man who inspects all of these docu-
ments. He will handle this matter for me."

He called for his aide and what do you think? The
aide was our Christian young man who had been
directing us step by step in the whole affair! He assured the governor that the document was in
proper order and that he concurred in the opinion
that we should have one of the buildings.

There was enough material from those buildings
for the church we had in mind, plus enough left
over for a second small church as well. We called a
man from the other location who had a boat and
he came and loaded up the leftover materials.

It was a miracle—but our God is able! I often
think of how He used that second American
colonel. He gave us food that they could not take
with them. For instance, he gave us several cases of
eggs—10 dozen eggs in a case. Believe me,
everyone all around us had eggs for many days.
Also, there were several great chunks of sausage in
long, stuffed cases.

We distributed it among hungry people and it
was a great joy. It gave us such encouragement to
be able to help the people. We had not stayed in
Japan in vain.

So, using the basic materials we had, we started to build the church. We went as far as we could with the limited funds we had on hand.

Then I said to Anne, "Let's go back up to Tokyo. I think we ought to have an audience with General MacArthur and see if he won't make a way for us to get some funds." We felt sure he would have something for us.

"Okay, let's go," Anne answered. "We can't do anything here without more money."

In Tokyo we met one of the Christian young men in the American forces with whom we had worked immediately after the surrender. He wanted us to tell him about our work and how it was going down in Matsuyama.

Then suddenly he said, "No, don't tell me now! Come to the meeting tonight so that all of the boys will have a chance to hear."

We accepted the invitation and that evening we told the young men about the needs and about the partial building of the church. One of the boys got up and, turning to the rest, said, "Say, we want to have a part in this, don't we?"

They took up an offering so that we could go back and continue with the church building. When they got through, we had the equivalent of 200,000 Japanese dollars, incredible as that may sound.

Well, of course, we didn't have to go and bother General MacArthur. We took our 200,000 Japanese dollars—a most gracious love offering from those Christian soldiers and sailors from America—and finished that little church building in Matsuyama without any debt!

18

Hiroshima

After completing the church at Matsuyama, we turned to Hiroshima, the center of our work before the war. The Bible school had been located there.

There was no place to stay in Hiroshima and I couldn't find anyone I knew. It was like a desolate wilderness. In the internment camp we had been told only that a terrible new weapon had been used against Japan. We did not know, at that time, that the atomic bomb had much to do with the end of the war.

Many have written since the war, about the horror and the suffering and the deaths at Hiroshima and Nagasaki. There was no escape, no getting out. Many saw their loved ones burned alive. Those in the center of the blast just disintegrated, with no trace of them left. Stones fused together. The concussion was so terrible that people's eyes stood right out on their cheeks, pulled right out of their heads. Many that were burned rushed to the river. The river was jammed with dead bodies.

A woman who was a preacher told of her experience as both she and her husband, also a preacher, were burned in the atomic blast.

She said, "I was lying there on the ground and I was sure that my husband must have been in the precinct at the explosion. I told those who came to help not to move me because my husband would come. Later, I leaned on my arm to look around. My husband was there, near me. He had been burned to death."

Hiroshima had been a great, beautiful city. But everything was destroyed. I couldn't find a thing, not even the street where our church and buildings had stood.

A Japanese soldier said, "I have been home three weeks. I cannot find any trace of my people."

A lady said, "I was out of town that morning, but I have never found any trace of my people. They are all gone."

On my third trip to Hiroshima, I found one of our Christian men who was trying to put up a shack on the main street so that he could get his little business started again. There was no space for me to stay overnight because they had only a little shelter over their heads. But he sent the children to relatives in the country and I stayed with them. The next day we found a piece of land on which our church in Hiroshima now stands.

The same questions arose: "What shall we do? How shall we begin?"

I went to our senior adviser, pastor and teacher— Rev. Kuniji Oye—who had been a keen, bright leader in the church before the war.

I told him about the purchase of the land and added, "But I can't build a church here and still live in Matsuyama."

"Let's take the whole matter to God," he advised. We got down and prayed and asked the Lord to give us someone to oversee the building and to pastor the Hiroshima church.

I don't have the space to tell you of the miraculous way in which the Lord led Mr. Oye's son to help us in the work. He is the Rev. Suteichi Oye, the president of the national church in Japan. Before the war, he had been a prominent pastor with another evangelical group in Japan. But he had been put in prison during the war because of his faith and his strong stand against the war and the military forces.

Weak and in ill health after his release, he had turned to business. But he still could not get away from the call to preach the gospel. We were so thrilled when he came to talk to us about the possibility of the ministry again in Hiroshima.

"I know of your work and your faith," I told him. "I would very much like to have you join us and take up the work in Hiroshima. But I can't offer you any salary, for I don't have one myself. I trust God for my living from day to day."

He said to me, "If you can trust God, I can trust Him, too! So I will come."

The problems multiplied. First of all, where would Mr. Oye live with his family? We had nothing except a piece of land.

Just at that time, Mr. Oye's uncle, who had been visiting in Japan and had been stranded there by the war, waiting for a visa to get back to America, gathered together enough materials to build himself a small, two-room building.

Suddenly his visa had come, and he said to our Mr. Oye, "Now, I've gathered this material and I am going to give it all over to you. You can build yourself a little shack to live in while you are building the church."

We had to go to the city offices and get permission to build a church. The officials were both puzzled and intrigued about the size of the church we were planning.

"Why do you want to build such a big church? How much money do you have for the project?" they asked.

"Well," I said, "to be honest with you, I have none. But I have faith in the living God."

They looked at me as if I were crazy and Mr. Oye said he didn't know what to think about one giving such an answer to the city officials.

In spite of my answer, I guess they thought they would try me and see how I came out. They gave me permission to build.

We called a carpenter and made the plans which included a small shack in which to keep his tools and to live while he was building. As the work progressed, the carpenter came to me and said, "Miss Francis, at the end of this month, I simply must have one thousand dollars American or I can't go on." (That would be 360,000 Japanese dollars.)

I felt like Peter sinking in the sea, but I prayed, "Lord, I don't know how to get that money, but don't let me sink now. I am already out of the boat. I have started."

At the end of the month I paid the carpenter $1,000, but I couldn't tell you now where it came from. I remember counting it out dollar by dollar, for there were no big bills then in Japanese money and it took 360 of those dollars to make one American dollar. What a great joy, finally, to be able to begin our services and invite the suffering, the hopeless, and the sad and mourning people to hear about the living God. I will never forget that first night. The church was large, but it was packed. How they listened as God gave us a message of comfort. And when we gave the altar call, down they came!

I remember a girl, a high-class girl, who had been burned from her nose down. From her nose up she was beautiful. She was so ashamed of her burns that she had not been going out in public. But a Christian friend had said to her that night, "I want you to go with me. We will sit in the back row and before the benediction is pronounced I will go out with you." Finally, she had consented to come.

Before the message was over, however, the light of God shone into that girl's heart. When the invitation was given, she didn't care what kind of a scarred face she had. She was looking for God.

She looked up through her tears and said, "I never thought I would ever thank God, or anybody, for these scars. But tonight, in the depths of my being, I thought that if this had not happened to me, I might never have heard this wonderful message of God. And I understand it!"

She was saved that night and she is in heaven now. She didn't live very long after that.

When the first meeting was over and nearly everyone was gone, I noticed a little woman standing at the side. She seemed to be wanting to say something. I went down and took her by the hand. "Oh, Sensei," she said, "I understood it! I got it!" She was thrilled. I asked her to sit beside me as she told me her story.

"That morning when the bomb struck," she said, "I was at my home up on the mountainside. My two little children were playing on the floor—a one-year-old and a three-year-old.

"I stooped down to pick up something and in that second the awful flash of light came. I was startled and stood up to look around. When I looked back, my two children were charred at my feet—both dead.

"I didn't know then that I was all burned. I was so concerned for my little ones. I picked them up and laid them aside. Pretty soon I began to feel the pain in my own body. Then I found how badly I was burned. I thought to myself, 'What terrible things have I done that this should happen to me? And what of my children who were here just a minute ago—and now they are not?'

"Oh, how I have suffered," she continued. "I have dragged my weary body to every shrine and every temple I could find. If I would hear of another, I would go. But nothing has brought me any comfort. I still did not know where the life of my children had gone.

"But tonight you told us of this God's love and that it was He who created us and you said my children are with Him. I believe it! I believe it! My heart is comforted. Light has come to me."

We prayed together and I believe she was saved that night.

Many would find it hard to believe the story of her own physical ailments after those burns. She told me how maggots would gather in the sores, for she had no bandages.

"I was just simply a living death," she told me.

Later her eyes were affected and a doctor told her there was no hope because of the aftereffect of the radiation.

She told Mr. Oye, "Even though the doctor said there is no help for me, I believe that the God who could save me can heal this! I want you to pray for me."

Mr. Oye prayed, and within three days her eyes were healed completely and she has had no trouble since.

Having gone this far at Hiroshima, I knew that if we really wanted to proceed with our work, we had to have a school for Bible teaching and pastoral training.

Mr. Oye's father was one of the best teachers I have ever met. He said he would help me with the school and the teaching. I traveled all through the country to see if I could find a house to rent, but there was nothing.

Finally, one night I was awake, unable to sleep for thinking about the need for a school. It seemed as though the Lord said to me, "Take that shack that the carpenter built for his tools. Even though it is small, there is an upstairs and a downstairs. And take the house that Mr. Oye lived in while this one was being built and put them together and make yourself a school!"

So that's what we did. Our school began in those shacks. The boys slept upstairs and the girls downstairs. Mr. Oye taught them and his son gave us part-time help even though he was busy with his pastoral work.

It was this school building which made Dr. Snead shake his head and exclaim, "This will never do!" By that time, the Alliance had decided to come back and Mr. McGarvey was field director. We hunted more than a year for a piece of land and finally found the property on which our school now stands.

19

A Special Place in My Heart

By this time you may have suspected that the women of Japan have a special place in my heart. Maybe that is partly due to the fact that I am a woman myself, but it is also due to their faithfulness and loyalty and to the manner in which the Christian women have stood by the work of God.

I have mentioned the great need for a Bible school so that we could train pastors and workers. The young women who have graduated from our school have done excellent work. Several have their own churches and are doing well as pastors and evangelists. Some of the girls, of course, are wives of pastors.

In spite of the many hardships that followed the end of the war, God gave us a wonderful ministry among the women. They were so broken down and so sad. They had struggled valiantly to keep their families alive. During the war and when food was so scarce, they had scraped and scrimped to get enough to keep their children in fair health and to clothe them. But such strain and such privations, along with the bitterness of national defeat, had left them depressed.

We found that they were very open to the message of the Christian gospel. Groups of women began to call us for meetings and discussions. It was interesting that the women wanted me to speak to them, while the men often called my sister because she had been a teacher and she seemed to understand better how to meet them and present the message.

There were so many calls from women in different sections that the government appointed an official to travel with me for planning and preparation. He would come and get me and take my bag and escort me to the place where I was to speak.

I was asked to come to one place where there was no public meeting place except a large Buddhist temple. The priest said, "It is all right. Come into the temple and speak here."

I was so short that the people couldn't see me when I stood. So the priest pulled out his desk—they sit on desks and let their robes hang down over the edge—and said to me, "Stand up here on my table."

So I stood on the priest's table inside the temple and proclaimed the gospel of our Lord Jesus Christ to those people. It became so that I could hardly step out of the house without someone running to meet me because they all knew me. When I would get on the train, someone would say, "Hello, here she is!" and everyone would nod to me.

I would go into the hospital to pray with some-

one, to visit the sick, and some would say to me,
"Oh, I heard you in such-and-such a town!" They
would all want me to come to their bedside and
pray for them.

More than four years had gone by after the war
and we were still living in that one little room that
had been opened to us in that solitary house left
standing in Matsuyama. One day I fell and hurt my
side very badly. While I was laid up in bed, the
Lord spoke to me and said, "It is time now to build
your own house."

We had been so very busy with our work and the
opportunities for witness that I hadn't really
thought beyond that one little room which had
been opened for us so miraculously.

"But, Lord," I said, "I have no money. How can I
build a house?"

And He said, "I'll look out for that. You go
ahead, call your carpenter, build the house and I
will see to the money."

Well, I obeyed and I called the carpenter. I was
going to find a piece of property away from the
church, but the pastor said, "You had better build
on the land that we have for the church. Then you
will be a part of it and you won't have taxes to pay."

So I built there. It was a large house. Every time
the bills came in, money came from somewhere.

It was right at that time that I heard from a dear
lady whom I had met years before in Minnesota.
She sent me a thousand dollars after the Lord had
promised that the money would come in for the
house. What a great encouragement that was!

When the house was finished, there was not a

penny of debt on it. Everything was paid for. And, oh, how nice to be able to go from room to room! We had been living in such a cramped place so long that I said to my sister, "Isn't it lovely to be able to stand in one room and look into another?"

That house enabled us to have two downstairs parlors that we could put together. We could have two classes at the same time, Anne teaching one class, while I taught the other. Or we could have them all in one large class.

We had English classes and women's classes there. Much of our work was carried on there at our own home. It is just wonderful how God can supply the need. He kept His word when He said, "I'll look out for that."

We opened a small work in Minara, about an hour from Matsuyama by train. The pastor in Matsuyama had been taking time out of his work for a cottage prayer meeting there, but I began to feel burdened to build there, so that the work could be separate from Matsuyama.

One of the Christians came to me one morning and said, "There is a wonderful piece of land in this section which can be bought at a very good price." We looked it over and bought it. By the time we came to build, we found that it was not quite enough.

Finally, a man heard about our dilemma and said, "I am not a Christian but I own some land. I want a church up here. I have perceived that wherever there is a Christian church, the standard of the community rises. I want a church in our village."

He made an offer to exchange sufficient property

on which to build the church for the first property
we had purchased. It was my vision and desire that
we should have both a church and a kindergarten.
With the teaching of evolution in the schools, I
thought the only way to help these children was to
give them a knowledge of God before they got into
the primary schools.

So I started a new ministry in kindergartens and
the Lord marvelously sent in the funds. Wherever I
went in evangelistic work, I received gifts. I put
them all aside and we finally had enough to begin
construction. I wanted this project to be built and
carried on with funds given by the Japanese. We
were able to put up a building large enough to
house the kindergarten project as well.

After the kindergarten had been in operation in
Minara for about a year, we held a service and
asked the father of one of the little boys in the class
to take part in the program. He could not speak
without tears as he said, "Today, in Japan, our
young people have no respect for anyone. When
my little boy was born, I made up my mind that I
would try to teach him respect if it took my
lifetime.

"When the kindergarten opened, I thought that it
might be a help, so I sent my small son. After he
had been attending the classes for a short time, we
were sitting down, as usual, for our evening meal. I
picked up my chopsticks and began to eat.

"But the boy said, 'Father, just a minute.' The little fellow then laid his chopsticks down and bowed
his head and thanked God for his food.

"You will never know how much that has meant

to me," the father continued. "I thought it would take my whole lifetime to teach him reverence, but he has learned it already!"

In another instance, a mother came to tell us of the intervention of her five-year-old son during a very severe argument between his mother and father. The little boy had learned Bible verses and Christian teaching in the kindergarten. He was playing on the floor as the parents were arguing. He got up and stood in front of them and said, "Forgiving one another, forgiving one another."

The mother, telling us about it, said, "We were so ashamed!"

When I left Japan, there were 93 children in the kindergarten adjoining my house, 93 children playing in my backyard every day, lively and noisy. But I loved them! I continued in my evangelistic ministries and Japanese young women ran the kindergarten.

20

"The Weary Ladies"

For years Anne and I had been known as "The Ladies" among our many Japanese friends and visitors. But during 1964, after Anne had been on the field 42 years and I was completing my 55th year in Japan, I think we should have been described as "The Weary Ladies."

My sister's ministry in Japan had been outstanding. She had mastered the Japanese language and was considered an authority even by the Japanese themselves. She had a most valuable ministry as a teacher. When the Alliance opened the Bible school again in Hiroshima after the war, Anne went there to help as a teacher.

When this load at the Bible school became too great for her physical strength, she came to live with me in Matsuyama. Together we launched the kindergarten project and the church group in Minara.

In 1964, Anne slipped and fell on the polished kindergarten floor. Some bones in her arm snapped right off. This ordeal severely tested her nerves and she was never really well after that. We tried to get her to rest, but she would say, "What's a little broken arm?"

Her health gradually declined. Her heart seemed to get worse. There were many nights that she couldn't get her breath. She would sit with her back up against me and I would plead in prayer and ask the Lord to touch her and give her breath. These were terrible nights for me because I had heart trouble, too.

We finally went to Kyoto to rest. We must have been a pitiful sight, for she was up one day and down the next and I was up the day she was down. Both Anne and I continued to pray in faith, expecting deliverance.

When I would ask the Japanese to pray for me, they would say, "Why, yes, we will pray for you, but don't forget your age!" They thought I ought to be willing to die since I was past 80 years of age! I said within myself, "Well, it is no use to depend on their prayers because they are just looking at my wrinkles instead of at God!"

So I began to pray by myself and God gave me an assurance from the experience of Sarah in the Old Testament that although she was past age, she judged Him faithful who had promised.

At that point I had the worst attack physically that I have ever had. For 48 hours the doctor said, "If we can't stop this, it is going to stop you!" All the while I was reminding the Lord, "Your Word cannot fail—it cannot fail! That's all there is to it. I am healed!" Since that attack I have not had another to this day. The Lord healed me.

Anne continued to fail during 1965. One morning the Lord said to me, "You must get ready to go home and take her away. This is too much for her."

An amazing thing happened in the Lord's provision. I had expected that when the time came, I could never pack my things and say farewell to Japan. I had thought, "I will just weep and weep!"

But when the time finally came to pack, I did not shed one tear. God's will filled my being and I went to work. Anne couldn't help. I packed all of our things myself and disposed of the items which had to be discarded and got ready to come home.

When the people found out that we were actually going to leave, there was quite a stir. The officials decided to make us honorary citizens of Japan and to bring us before the public in a special ceremony.

When I found out that the committee had hired the largest auditorium in the city of Matsuyama—a great hall built since the war—I was upset. I was thinking about the expense. But they wanted to do it. They decorated it and called the people in. My job was to tell why I'd come to Japan in the first place and why we stayed through thick and thin all these many years.

One man composed an ode to us, explaining that we came over bright and young and fair, like flowers, and that we had stayed there with them until we were withered and had to go home!

It was a real privilege to tell them the secret of it all. And I poured out my heart if ever I did!

The choir from a girls' school sang the "Hallelujah Chorus." Afterward, the entire group sang, "God Be with You Till We Meet Again." There was weeping everywhere.

When we came home after the ceremony, the

Christian ladies who had been praying for this opportunity of witness were excited and gratified. "It
wasn't like a ceremony at all," they said. "It was just
like a revival meeting."

Then all of the Christian missionaries in the area
and the churches had their own service of farewell.

I had opportunity several times to tell the
Japanese officials and leaders that "God has
created you, the Japanese nation. There are no
other people like you. You are a peculiar nation
and God has an intense love for you. He has a purpose for you." I went on to show them what they
could do for the world if they loved God.

"The reason Japan is hemmed in in this little island is because you haven't the love that goes out
and loves the world," I reminded them.

On the day of our departure from Japan, Septem-
ber 6, 1965, hundreds came to the airport. The
farewells started all over again—and the tears as
well.

As usual, the Lord had gone before and had
prepared a home for us in Toledo, Ohio, where
Tom had lived up to the time of his death and
where Anne and I had lived during our furlough in
1962.

When our friends in Toledo heard that "The
Weary Ladies" were about to come home, Mr. and
Mrs. George McLean said, "Our basement apartment is being vacated and we will not rent it out
again. We will get busy and fix it up for the missionary ladies. They can have it for their home as
long as they need it."

Meanwhile, of course, Anne and I had talked

about our situation. We had no definite plan worked out for a permanent residence in the States.

Finally arriving at Toledo, we were surprised to find a crowd of friends and well-wishers waiting for us at the airport. It was such a lovely time of greetings and fellowship.

"Thank you for coming," we finally said, "but we must bid you all good night!" We couldn't really have told anyone exactly where we were going for the night!

Someone said, "Oh, we have a place for you to stay." So they all came with us to the McLean home and it was a real housewarming. They took us through the rooms and said, "This is your home—don't look any farther!"

I wonder if anyone can fully realize what that meant to us?

The McLeans had fixed the apartment so beautifully and our friends had sent in food for the refrigerator and for the cupboards. The beds were all made up and there were red rosebuds in a vase to make our welcome complete.

And so we were "at home." The McLeans told us there would be no rent to pay—that this would be a part of their missionary offering. Our only responsibility was a small charge for utilities each month. We were so grateful! And we were so comfortable!

Anne did not regain her strength. During those weeks of fall and early winter in 1965, her only activity was the activity of prayer for the field and for the loved ones in Japan.

On the morning of December 28 we had a lovely time in prayer. Anne seemed brighter and stronger. While we were eating lunch, she read a letter from Pastor Fujika in Japan. She started to reach for another letter when she collapsed and fell to the floor.

I rushed to her, but she was gone. Like Enoch, she did not see death. She opened her eyes and it was heaven!

Some have asked what I thought she was doing up in heaven and I had to reply, "Well, I don't know, but I'm almost sure that the first thing she did was to go and tell Jesus that He would have to care for me now!"

And He has been doing that faithfully day by day!

Epilogue

The Japanese people in their darkest hours caught a realistic glimpse of the saving grace and the compassionate love of Jesus Christ, the Savior of the world. The saw the gospel of Christ walking about in their ruined streets in the person of Miss Mabel Francis.

Many of their lives were brought into relationship with Jesus Christ, through faith in Him, because of her testimony and declaration of the Word of God that they, too, could become children of God through the miracle of the new birth.

She told them faithfully, "There is a better way than you have known. Put your faith in Him, the living and the true God, and the meaning of existence will no longer be a puzzle to you!"

In 1962 when she had reached the age of 81 but had scarcely slowed down in her energetic career of preaching, teaching and concern for the Japanese people, Miss Francis was asked to appear before the nation's highest officials.

The governor of the prefecture in which she had lived and taught the Christian gospel for so many years had asked the Japanese government and the Emperor of the nation to honor her for her contribution "to the welfare of the Japanese people in their distress and confusion at the time of their defeat," and for "the long years spent in leading hundreds of Japanese to the knowledge of God, to peace of heart and mind."

The little American lady who had become more and more like her adopted Japanese with each year that passed was smiling as the ceremony took place, but she could hardly believe what she heard.

Standing in the presence of representatives of the Emperor, she was presented with a beautiful parchment scroll bearing the Emperor's seal and detailing her services to the Japanese people. Then she was given an unusual gold medal, conferring upon her the unique honor of membership in the highly exclusive Fifth Order of the Sacred Treasure.

With this token of friendship and regard, Japanese officialdom implied that Miss Francis could now consider herself a Japanese citizen and since that time, in special functions of state, a place of honor has been reserved for her as a member of the Order.

The true nature of this honor is revealed by the fact that this once feared and widely despised Christian missionary is the first person in Japanese history to have received the medal of the Fifth Order of the Sacred Treasure while still alive. Prior to this award ceremony in 1962, it had been the custom of the Emperor to bestow the medal as the highest civilian award on Japanese who had served their country in some unusual way—but who had also passed on into eternity!

"Why have I been chosen?" Miss Francis asked herself.

After the war, she had helped to feed the hungry and she had visited those who were sick. She visited others who were in prison. She took the children to her heart and worked to better their conditions and their opportunities.

But the Governor of Ehime Prefecture, Sadatake Hisamatsu, who had stepped down from a position of nobility to become active in political leadership after the war, took into account the example of her Christian faith.

"She gave both materially and spiritually to the welfare of the Japanese people," he said, "especially at the close of the war in the time of defeat when the Japanese people were in extreme distress and bewilderment. She traveled widely and gave unprecedented assistance and encouragement to our people by her Christian faith."

Much earlier—actually, in 1949—a Japanese young man who was looking for the living God said it simply when he came to Miss Francis in Matsuyama and told her: "About the time I became old enough to think for myself, the teaching of our schools was controlled by war propaganda. Then the war ended and all was lost. All that I had been taught was shattered.

"I felt crazed. I wanted to do everything that was bad. I was so disobedient and profligate that I even beat my old father and mother.

"I got to the end of my rope. One night in my misery, I climbed the mountain near my home. I stood there and screamed out at the moon, but there was no help. I cried out to the forest, but only the echo of my own voice came back.

"Then I thought of the church. I did not know about God, but I thought I would go to the church anyway. I waited until no one was looking and entered secretly and tried to pray. I did not know to whom I was praying, but my heart became quiet.

"I went home and apologized to my parents. They said, 'We have waited for this day,' and they wept for joy.

"I determined to be a true man. I did not know Jesus but I made a wooden cross and put it on my desk and tried to do right.

"Now you tell me of the living Christ. This, oh, this is what I have waited for!"

In her prayer letter of February, 1949, Mabel Francis added: "Praise God for such ripe fruit to pick for the Master. I come home from my trips tired but rejoicing. After two days' rest, I will be starting out in another direction with my sister."

Small wonder that there was always something more for her to do in Japan. Small wonder that she took only a brief furlough in the United States in 1962 and returned to her life work in Japan at the age of 83!

Mabel Francis continued her effective retirement ministry from coast to coast, even when she reached her 87th birthday on July 26, 1967, urging Christian young people to consider service in Japan, which she has had to relinquish.

In a Life Investment Conference for young people of The Christian and Missionary Alliance, a television news reporter referred to Miss Francis as "a livin' doll."

"Bring that young man back," she said when she heard about it, "Tell him that I'm an old war horse, with still a lot to get done for the Lord!"

Appendix I

A Legend in Her Time

By Anita M. Bailey

S he was a legend in her time, this indomitable little woman with shining eyes and a seemingly perpetual smile.

This is the story of Miss Mabel Francis, who was a teenage preacher before the turn of the century, who spent 56 years in Japan, whose life touched high officials and humble peasants, who had friends among cultured ladies and girls of the street, who received the highest award Japan ever gave a living person and who went into war hospitals and prisons with the message of love and hope.

For 79 of her nearly 95 years she served the Lord. Who can measure the impact of her life? Her testimony was always convincing. Age never mattered, young people especially were charmed by her simplicity, and they loved her for revealing Christ.

The Lord called her to Himself on June 7, 1975 just days after a visit from Rev. Kozo Tamura and Rev. Shigeo Kuwahara, beloved Japanese co-workers who had attended the Alliance World Fellowship meeting. They returned to Japan with the hush of God's presence and the glow of her benediction upon them.

Surely she is now enjoying the presence of the Lord, for she talked of Him continually and lived only to tell others how He could dwell in their hearts and give victory and peace in any circumstance. Such a life came from dying to self, she said, and death is never easy. But to have the life of Christ within was worth it all. She could say with Paul: "I am crucified with Christ, nevertheless I live: yet not I, but Christ liveth in me."

She was years learning this lesson, but it was the greatest experience of her life, she said. As a child she had given her heart to the Lord. At the age of 15, she received the Holy Spirit and then, while teaching school in a rural community in her home state of New Hampshire, God told her to share the news of His love with the people in the area. She preached on Sunday afternoons in the schoolhouse.

Several years later, while attending a farewell meeting for a couple going to Japan and praying for others to go, God called her to His service. Almost 10 years later, after attending what is now Gordon College, Defiance (Ohio) College and A.B. Simpson's missionary training school at Nyack, as well as working in a rescue mission in Brockton, Massachusetts, she was ready.

No missionary took an elaborate "outfit" in 1909, but the one Miss Francis took must have been the smallest any missionary ever had: her little steamer trunk contained some cutlery, a few books, some mementos of her family, a half-pound of cocoa and three cotton dresses. When she arrived she could wear only two of the dresses—she discovered the black-and-white check of the third was a pattern worn only by men in Japan!

In 1909 Miss Francis was conspicuous in Japan, and also suspect. Parents taught their children to fear this foreigner. Adults, though always polite, kept her at a distance. After her successful public ministry in North America, this resistance was a great test of her dedication. Perseverance and love won out, however, and as she traveled (by bicycle) and preached and served the people, they did respond. Eventually she and her brother, who joined her in 1913, established 20 churches. In 1924 her widowed sister, Mrs. Anne Dievendorf, also went to Japan, and for the next 40 years their work complemented each other's. Mabel evangelized and Mrs. Dievendorf held Bible classes.

The years of the Depression brought two great crises to Miss Francis. One was the decision of the Alliance to terminate missionary work in Japan. Called to Japan by God, could she trust Him to supply all her needs, "even if she lived to be 70 and people forgot about her"? She decided she must, and she and her sister remained independently.

The second crisis transformed her life, for it was then she learned how to appropriate the life of Christ. Though she had received the Holy Spirit in her youth, she supposed that holiness came through eradication of sin in the heart. Yet she was constantly plagued with what she knew were sins: impatience, irritability, self-consciousness, pride, concern for her reputation and her rights. At last she found the secret. "I began to see that everything God allowed to come into my life had a purpose. If He allowed someone to be rude to me, the question was not about that person but about how I would react."

God brought one thing after another to her attention, and then in this humbling experience His Word came: "If we have been planted together in the likeness of his resurrection."

"It just seemed then like death was over and I was in the resurrection life," she wrote. "It was no more I, but Christ."

She loved to quote Dr. Simpson's poem: "The change is not in me,/ Rather, it seems that He/ Has come Himself to live His life in mine;/ And as I stepped aside/ And took Him to abide./ He came and filled me with His life divine." But it was not a once-for-all experience, she learned; it was a continuing process of death and life. This became her life message.

The war years in Japan were hard. First came house arrest for 12 months and then three years of internment with much privation. At the end she was 64 years old and had been in Japan 36 years—with only two furloughs. But it was not time to retire. Rather, she entered into her greatest ministry. Hundreds found Christ, among them many American servicemen.

Many honors came to this unassuming little woman. In 1962, in appreciation for her contribution "to the welfare of the Japanese people in their distress and confusion at the time of their defeat," and for "the long years spent in leading hundreds of

Japanese to the knowledge of God, to peace of heart and mind," she received from the Emperor of Japan membership in the exclusive Fifth Order of the Sacred Treasure, the first person in Japanese history to receive this highest civilian honor while still alive.

In 1965 "the ladies" knew it was time to leave Japan. Miss Francis was 84. It was then she received, in public ceremonies, the key to Matsuyama, the city where she had ministered to so many for so long.

But God commissioned her for still a new ministry, sharing the message of victory in Christ with North American Christians. She traveled widely with much blessing.

Still, Japan was her first love. Invited in 1969 to share in the 20th anniversary services of the reestablished Alliance Church, Miss Francis (then 88) planned a five-month visit to her people. The opportunities of ministry stretched to a full 10 months before she returned to the homeland, her heart still burning with love. "Oh, the need I felt!" she wrote. "Had I been younger, nothing would have induced me to leave."

Weakness, following an operation in 1972 for a cancer on her lip, finally persuaded her to retire to Shell Point Village in Florida. Even in these late years she found the strength to speak occasionally, and she put her experience into a book: *Filled With the Spirit . . . Then What?* (Christian Publications).

There was a glorious memorial service in Fort Myers, with Dr. Richard H. Harvey bringing a gospel message. Dr. W.F. Smalley spoke on behalf of the Society and the thousands whose lives she had touched, and Rev. A. Paul McGarvey gave intimate glimpses into her life in Japan and her Christian character. A number of others took part, and 30 missionaries and pastors from Shell Point Village formed an honor guard.

Worthy of honor, Mabel Francis would give it all to her Lord whom she loved supremely all her life.

(Taken from The Alliance Witness, *July 30, 1975. Used by permission.)*

Appendix II

Better than a Fable

By Gladys M. Jasper

The life of Mutsuko Yoneda could have been a once-upon-a-time story. It began many years ago when a young American woman heard the call of God to leave home and family to serve Him in a distant land. In the course of time, after years of training and preparation, this young foreigner found herself adjusting to life in Japan.

Her devotion to Jesus and her concern for people eventually brought her into contact with Mutsuko Yoneda, the young daughter of a town mayor in Hiroshima. That contact brought Mutsuko into a personal relationship with Jesus Christ. Given Mutsuko's social standing and financial security, her story should continue that she married and lived happily ever after. Such was not to be.

Still, her life reads better than a fable.

This young Japanese Christian soon felt that the Lord was also calling her to be a missionary. In her case, however, it was not possible for her to make an independent decision as the American missionary had done. Mutsuko learned that her parents had already arranged a marriage for her with a non-Christian man. She was disconsolate, but family counsel prevailed. She was eventually assured in her heart that even in this the Lord could work all things together for her good.

The years passed, and three little girls were born—Yasuko, Takako and Naoko. All seemed to be going well when one day the mother was called to bring her three children and to appear at the municipal office. There she learned that her husband had died for the Emperor in World War II.

What tragedy! What could a lone widow with three daughters do to earn a living and protect her children? The horror of it beat through Mutsuko's brain.

In desperation she decided the only way out was to end life for all of them. Thus, while traveling back to Hiroshima by train, she determined that when they sped over the large railway bridge she would open the door, push her children out and then jump out after them. That would settle everything!

Suddenly a thought flashed through Mutsuko's mind which she recognized to be the voice of God. "You wanted to be a missionary, didn't you? Can't you train these girls to be missionaries for me?"

Stunned, the young widow realized the enormity of what she had contemplated and asked the Lord to forgive her. She promised to rear her daughters to follow Him.

Back went Mutsuko to her home in Hiroshima, but now there was a somewhat lighter step in her walk. Her doctor sister-in-law employed her as a dietician in her clinic. There she was loved and well treated. Life began to seem good once more.

Then the Lord began to speak to Mutsuko again, this time bringing to her attention the words of Genesis 19:17. "Escape to the mountain." Disturbed by this, she eventually asked her sister-in-law for permission to leave. Naturally the doctor was surprised and asked what was wrong. She told her that if a higher salary were required it could be provided, or if there were anything else needed, it could be arranged. Mutsuko attempted to forget the insistent words ringing in her ears, "Escape to the mountain, escape to the mountain."

But three months later she could stand it no longer. Again she appealed to the doctor to let her go, saying it was her God who had told her to act. This time the doctor readily agreed and said that if her God ordered her thus, she must obey.

Early the next morning the atom bomb dropped on Hiroshima. The clinic that had once provided shelter and employment was flattened. When the rubble was removed, only the doctor was found—safe in a depression under tons of debris, but scarred for life by radiation.

In the course of time Mutsuko married Minoru Hasegawa, a submarine captain who had helped sink an aircraft carrier at Pearl Harbor. He was now converted and living for the Lord. The three girls grew up determined to follow the Lord as He should lead. One by one they went off to the Emmanuel Bible Training College.

One day three fine young men—all trained at Emmanuel and then graduated from Union Biblical Seminary in Yeotmal, India, returned to the land of their birth and in a triple ceremony married the three sisters. What joy and rejoicing there was that day!

In a short time the three young couples found themselves in the place of God's appointing. Rev. and Mrs. Stephen Tanaka are missionaries in Kenya; Rev. and Mrs. Philip Hirai serve in Jamaica; and Rev. and Mrs. Joshua Tsutada are on the faculty of Union Biblical Seminary in India.

But that is not the end of the story.

When Joshua was home on furlough in Japan recently, he gave a missionary message, followed by an appeal for service. There was a gratifying response, but something caught his attention. From one side of the church he saw a white-haired lady come forward. Mutsuko and her husband—making independent and separate decisions—still wanted their lives to count for missions.

Mutsuko and her husband today serve at the home base, helping others fulfill their call overseas. Through the faithfulness of a mayor's young daughter, years before, seven others knelt in obedience to serve Christ in Japan and on three different continents.

And what of the lady who started the whole chain of response? Perhaps Miss Mabel Francis does not know of this result of her following hard after Jesus. But there will be those from Jamaica and from India who will rise up and call her blessed because of her faithfulness.

(*Taken from* The Alliance Witness, *February 27, 1974. Used by permission.*)

Appendix III

Interview with Miss Mabel Francis, age 92, submitted by Mrs. Eunice Wilkinson, Toledo, Ohio.

EW: When did you arrive in Japan?

MF: I arrived in Japan in 1909. Towards the last of November. I had wonderful victory. The anointing of God came upon me. And it wasn't me. It was the Holy Spirit working. I knew very little about the Holy Spirit, although sometimes I thought I was the one doing the work. But it was God. When I went finally to Japan, why, I thought I had a pretty good experience. I thought I knew something about the will of God. But when I got there, and everything was so different and I couldn't talk to anybody, now the inspiration was gone. I couldn't say a word. Nobody understood me. I studied hard because I thought, "This is what I've got to do if I'm going to preach to these people."

While I was studying like that, I found what I really was. I just couldn't understand it. I had supposed that the baptism of the Holy Ghost would be a victory all the way through. Now I didn't have victory. I was all upset about things. You see, when I was speaking at home, nobody quite knew me.

Everybody was afraid of me. Souls were being saved. Things were moving along fine. And now I couldn't say a word to anybody. Everything was all changed and I found I got sick. I got impatient. I got out of sorts. I felt very much downcast.

Then I went to the Lord about this. And I said, "Lord, I don't understand. I supposed that when the Holy Spirit came into my heart that all these things were gone and here they are. I'm impatient, I'm upset, I'm hurt when people say things they shouldn't say."

The Lord said to me, "You would suppose that the baptism of the Holy Spirit would take away this self-life?"

Now, I had never really sensed the self-life before. They had called it the carnal nature. But I now sensed this other person within me.

The Lord said to me, "You must let this die, it is the only way to get rid of it."

But I said, "Lord, I don't know how to die. What do you mean by dying?"

Now, I knew He didn't mean my physical man. I knew it was this old Adam within, this self-life.

And He said, "This must die."

Then I said, "Teach me to die."

And He said, "The only way to die is to bring [the self-life] directly to me. I will place it on the cross. I will bring it to death. But you must bring it to me without any excuse, without explanation. So don't say it was because somebody else was so mean that you got upset or somebody else was crying, 'I am upset.' It's you I'm dealing with. I want you to bring it to me. Don't make any excuse for it."

I had been making excuses because people were saying things that were not nice. I thought they were to blame.

He said, "No, if you didn't have that nature there, it wouldn't stir it up, so that must be dealt with." So I just took it to Him. I would try to do exactly what He told me. Every time I would see any of this nature I would bring it directly to Him. He kept bringing experiences into my life and they showed up what I was.

EW: Miss Francis, when was it you came home to the States from Japan to stay here?

MF: In 1965.

EW: What have you been doing since you came home? Traveling?

MF: On the way back, God spoke to me again on the plane. "I have a new commission for you. I want you to go home and go from church to church and tell the people what I have taught you, what I have done for you. Tell them of the selfish nature." So I began, as soon as I could, to go about. And I found that, oh, how people need it!

EW: Miss Francis, how can young women be encouraged to realize that they can find great fulfillment in life apart from a family life?

MF: You don't have any say about it. You have to trust God. And God knows. I thought I could be married. Of course, that's a natural thing. The Lord said to me, "No, that's not coming in your life. I have another plan for you." From that time on it wasn't any problem. I knew I wasn't to be married.

EW: Recently, Miss Francis, you had to have some surgery and I was wondering if you wanted to share medically what was involved before the surgery and then, after that, you could share what the Lord has taught you, the blessings that have come from this experience.

MF: Well, you know I have always trusted God with my body. From a little child, in our home, if one of the children was ill, Mother put everything else aside and just prayed that the child would get well. And I was healed many, many times. In fact, I never saw anything else. So when this sore came on my lip, why I never thought of anything else but to trust in God. The doctor said, "You should have that operated on." But, I went on and on. It was seven years, until finally when I came back from Hawaii, I was very tired.

[The sore] began to eat. Until then it hadn't eaten very much—it had just been a sore on the top. But it ate down until almost half of my lip on one side was gone. Something had to be done. Either God had to touch me or I would have to go to surgery. It's not glorifying to God for me to let it go on like that. And I wanted to glorify God. I wanted His Name to be praised.

I said to Nancy, "I am troubled. I don't know what to do. I kept looking to the Lord, expecting

Him to do something. I'd get up here in the night for a couple of hours or more, reading my Bible and praying. And I would get such wonderful promises from God. The pain would be taken away and I would go back to sleep again. And I thought, *Well, He's surely working.* But it kept right on eating down.

So then I made up my mind. I don't think I had any special guidance. If I had, it would have been easier. I didn't. I just felt it was the thing to do. So I went to see the doctor. I had already met him.

He said, "I am very glad you came." I had perfect peace. I didn't have a word that said, "Go and get operated on." But I had peace. The operation was not painful. I didn't know anything about it. The only thing I knew was the first little prick of the anesthesia and I was out. I didn't wake up till it was all over.

EW: Miss Francis, some people ask, "Why do Christians suffer?" Would you like to share some of the things you've learned?

MF: Well, I don't know why Christians suffer. In fact, I don't ask. "Thy will be done," is all I say. We know that Jesus learned obedience through suffering. I have learned many lessons of inner quietness and trust. I don't know if I've learned so many outside things, but you just have to go deeper and deeper into God. That's what He's doing now—deepening down and deepening down.

You see, we are the bride of Christ and He wants us without spot, wrinkle or anything. You don't know what it takes to get the wrinkles out. You don't know what it takes to take the spots out. But He does. And He's working on something, and He doesn't always tell you what He's working on. My heart has great peace and joy and rest in Him.

EW: Now, what are your hopes and plans for the days ahead? What are some things you would like to do?

MF: Follow Him. I have told Him, "Now Lord, I don't know what you want. Do you want me to go on traveling and speaking or do you want me to be quiet and more in prayer, or what? You guide, because you are the King." So I am just waiting to hear from Him. And what ever He tells me, that I do.

Appendix IV

The following incidents were submitted by persons who knew Miss Mabel Francis and who cherish those memories.

Right after Japan surrendered, a group of young men from Youth for Christ came to Tokyo for an evangelistic campaign. They asked Mabel Francis to be the interpreter. As Miss Francis tells it, "These nice young men with their bow ties preached their American-oriented sermons. As they began to preach, I realized that they knew nothing of the Japanese culture.

"I knew they would never reach the Japanese people with their message. I also knew that they did not understand Japanese. So I let them preach their fine sermons in English and I preached my own sermon in Japanese.

"The Japanese, who did not understand English, did not know the difference. And the nice American boys who did not know Japanese did not know the difference. The only one who knew was my sister, and she did not say a word!"

Rev. Hann Browne
Santa Ana, California

Mabel Francis visited our congregation in the fall of 1971. Her health was already failing and we knew she had to have a light speaking agenda. Each afternoon she took a long nap and each evening she retired early.

Even so, I could see that my Sunday school class of junior high girls were enormously impressed with this tiny, but forceful woman. I wanted them to have some personal memory of her because I realized her mortal days were numbered.

Miss Francis agreed to give me one special message which I in turn would duplicate for each student, together with a picture of her from the advertising literature.

Here is the message in her own handwriting:

> Thy Will,
>   nothing more,
>   nothing less,
>   nothing else,
>
> When I was a girl I saw this motto on the desk of a friend. It has influenced my whole life so I give it to this group of dear girls.
>
>   Mabel Francis.

Jane Kenney
Campbell, New York

Miss Francis had been invited to be the featured speaker during the Beulah Beach Bible and Missionary Conference.

Her allotted time was to be 20 to 30 minutes, but she "waxed eloquent" for over an hour, on that hot afternoon in the tabernacle, after all the other features of the rally.

After supper in the cafeteria, I sat chatting with her for a few minutes and she told me that her friend, who had brought her to Beulah Beach from Toledo and with whom she was rooming in the hotel, wanted to attend the evening service that Sunday, but that she (Mabel) was going to go back to their room to rest instead.

"Betty likes to sit in all the meetings, but I don't—unless I'm doing the talking!"

Ruth E. Clark
Toledo, Ohio

During the spring of 1974 I received that much desired, although unrequested, missionary convention tour in Florida. It was my privilege to be sent to the Cape Coral church, so I was able to visit Shell Point Village and see several friends there. I had never met Mabel Francis prior to this time, so I was thrilled to visit her in the nursing center where she had recently been admitted.

This was during one of the special energy crises when all waste was pinpointed and deplored. As we visited, Mabel Francis called our attention to a stack of paper dinner napkins neatly cut in fourths and folded. Revealing her inborn Yankee thrift, she commented, "See, they bring another napkin at every meal. Wipe, throw, wipe, throw. No wonder there are shortages these days. I just cut these and save them, so I never need to buy Kleenex."

Olive Kingsbury
Cavendish, Vermont

When I first met Mabel Francis, I was going through deep problems and testing times. My husband was involved in an activity that caused me much stress and sorrow.

I suggested that we visit Miss Francis and he agreed. On one visit she laid her hands on his head and prayed such a loving and burdened prayer for him that it brought tears to his eyes.

Not long after that experience, he accepted the Lord. In 1970 he died and is now with the Lord. God answered her prayer.

Mrs. Rachel Webb
Toledo, Ohio

Our family was honored to have had some contact with Miss Mabel Francis. Our first memory is when Bob and I saw Mabel and her sister, Anne Dievendorf, step onto the Nyack chapel platform. Before either of them spoke, there were tears in the eyes of many students. You could hear the sniffles throughout the audience. The Spirit of God was upon these two saintly ladies.

Lois Long
Warren, Ohio

The following three paragraphs are excerpted from personal letters written by Mabel Francis to Elfriede Schaeffer, Cleveland, Ohio, and submitted by her:

"I wish I could tell you, my dear friends, how I was cheered and encouraged when you told me of the blessing the little book has been to you. This dying to self is not easy, but it is so wonderful to be dead and all through our inner being only to hear the voice of Jesus. Oh, if we could only tell it so that people would be willing to surrender all."

"The first of March I was taken very ill and went down to death's door. But Jesus came to me and said, 'I still have work for you. I cannot take you yet.' And from that day I began to get better. Now, I am quite well, only I tire very easily."

"There is a verse in Deut. 28:13, 'Thou shalt be above only, thou shalt not be beneath.' This word has been a great comfort. When the devil tries to put me under a cloud, I go to this word and say, 'I will not go under the devil's old cloud,' and I begin to praise the Lord. And soon I am on top up on the cloud! May He keep you 'above only'."

DATE DUE

The Library Store   #47-0103